MAGIC CASEMENTS

OTHER BOOKS BY THE SAME AUTHOR

Poetry

>TIME'S TRAVELERS
>GARNERED SHEAVES
>THE PAGEANT OF MAN
>GREEN VISTAS
>FROM A WESTERN HILLTOP
>WINDS OF CHAOS
>ARMAGEDDON
>THE LONE ADVENTURER
>SHADOWS ON A WALL
>THE ENDURING FLAME
>SONGS OF THE REDWOODS
>THE MOUNTAIN OF THE SLEEPING MAIDEN
>THE MERRY HUNT AND OTHER POEMS
>SENATOR GOOSE AND OTHER RHYMES
>THE THINKER AND OTHER POEMS

Prose

>THE RISE OF THE ANTI-POETS
>AN EDITOR LOOKS AT POETRY
>NEW POETIC LAMPS AND OLD
>THE LITERARY REVOLUTION
>FROM ARROW TO ATOM BOMB
>MARCHING MEN
>THE DECLINE OF MAN
>THE ANSWER OF THE AGES
>VILLAINS AND VIGILANTES
>THE SUNKEN WORLD
>THE WONDER STICK
>AFTER 12,000 YEARS
>THE PLANET OF YOUTH
>INTO PLUTONIAN DEPTHS
>WHEN THE BIRDS FLY SOUTH
>THE TRIUMPH OF THE TEAPOT POET

Anthologies

>UNSEEN WINGS
>THE MUSIC MAKERS
>MODERN AMERICAN LYRICS
>MODERN BRITISH LYRICS

Magic Casements

A GUIDEBOOK FOR POETS

by

STANTON A. COBLENTZ

1957

THE WINGS PRESS

Mill Valley   California

Copyright 1957

by

Stanton A. Coblentz

Printed in the United States of America
Library of Congress Catalog Card Number 57-12110

Contents

MAGIC CASEMENTS

I

Introduction: Is Confusion Necessary?

Sometimes I wonder what would happen to a Spenser or a Shakespeare, a Milton, a Shelley or a Keats born into the modern world. Endowed with pre-eminent poetic gifts, he would move in an environment where poetic gifts were not valued. Impelled to write rhythmically and majestically, he would find rhythm scorned by those who sat in criticism, and majesty contemned. Capable of crying out with a vibrant emotion and soaring to cloud-peaks of the imagination, he would be told that emotion should be put under harness, and imagination confined to the little conceits of a contrived originality. Inspired by a sense of wonder, filled with those dreams that are the substance of a poet's life, and swept by a passion for beauty, he would be slapped down with the assertion that wonder was out of date, that dreams were suitable enough for a simple-minded earlier age, and that beauty was among the unmentionables.

Would it be at all surprising if a Spenser or a Shakespeare, a Milton, a Shelley or a Keats became just a little confused in the face of such contradictions? And would the poet, one asks, cling to poetry at all, or would he turn to its easier rival prose, in view of the dilemma that confronted him—the choice of denying the impulses storming within his breast, or of flouting the tendencies of his age, and of being flouted by it in turn?

Now it is too much, of course, to assume that any fledgling Shakespeare, Milton or Keats is trying to lift his wings among us. On the other hand, we do know that many young poets are preparing to take flight—and we do not know, and by the nature of the circumstances cannot know, the extent of their untested ability. One thing we cannot deny is that they are entering a bewildering world, a world whose political, social and economic transformations are matched by its artistic shifts and befuddlements. If they glance to the right, they see the massive achievements of thirty centuries, peak piled upon peak in the literatures of many lands—poet following poet, great light shining behind great light, from Homer to de la Mare; and they note that each of these outstanding figures obeyed a tradition, from which he may have departed at times but which he never wholly abandoned. But if our young poets of today glance to the left, what do they observe? That the craftsmanship, the accumulated knowledge, the skills of three thousand years are flouted as absolutely as any Marxist regime ever berated "bourgeois religion" and western capitalism. What, then, shall our young poet choose?

Inevitably, he wants to be considered "modern." Inevitably, he wishes to be progressive. Inevitably, he has no respect for white hairs simply because they are white, nor for wrinkled faces because they are wrinkled. Quite properly, he desires to discard all that has been worn out, all that has outlasted its usefulness. If he pauses to consider, he will see that he is balanced on a steep ridge, with the peril of a fall on either side. On the one hand, he may accept the petrified prescriptions, the dogmas of a past that is overdue for interment; but on the other hand, he may bind himself by the ironclad regulations of a present that is untried and that may be discredited and scorned tomorrow or the day after. Which way shall he turn? What choice shall he make? Shall he pick the middle path? But often there is no middle path; and even if there is, it may represent that sort of compromise which is the first refuge of a coward, and may merely put off the eventual decision.

The problem is one of which I, personally, have long been aware. Having watched the poets and the poetry of nearly a quarter of a century from the vantage point of the editorial chair of a quarterly verse magazine, I have been in a position to note the doubts, the confusions and the changes that have overcome many. I have wondered what my own feelings would be if I, like an unknown number, were attempting my own poetic burgeonings in the Nineteen Fifties. I have felt the need experienced by young poets, as well as by many not so young, for guidance through the mazes of our times, in which they must inevitably run the gauntlet between the old and the new. And I have been impressed, above all, by the necessity for clear principles, assured standards, a firm and thoughtful approach to the matter of poetic values. Is confusion necessary? I do not for a moment believe so. But confusion is unavoidable in the absence of pilotage between the waste-land and the Promised Land. And such pilotage has conspicuously not been provided—not, at least, to anything like the required extent.

It would be presumptuous of me or of any man to suggest that a single-handed effort can fill the hiatus. But it would be negligent of anyone with convinced ideas and long experience not to make the try. I will not deny that I have definite convictions about poetry, present and past, and that these convictions are certain to affect the complexion of what I say; but I make bold to add that the bane of the age, both in literature and in general affairs, has been the man without convictions, the man who drifts with every current and shifts with every wind. Such views as I do have are built upon years of devotion to poetry, as critic, reader, verse-writer, anthologist, editor, and correspondent and friend of poets; and while I may err in my judgments, I am not without roots in my subject-matter.

Hence I offer these pages in the hope that they may provide guidance and assistance to the poet who stands bewildered amid the conflicts of the age—the poet who hardly knows whether the Parnassian meadows he seeks may be found along the wide, traveled road dipping to the left or the steep and lonely trail meandering to the right.

II

Music and Meter

We have no record of where and when the first human beings used articulate language. But we may be sure that their speech was confined to the simplest, most direct utterances: monosyllables like *Wurr, Gurr,* and *Urr,* meaning perhaps, "Watch Out!" "Run!", and "I'm hungry!" It may have been thousands of years before language served some purpose other than to name concrete objects and utilitarian needs, and before a vehicle was developed to express thought, emotion and imagination, and so to make the primitive beginnings of literature—a literature that, from the day of its origin, was a thing shining and wondrous, since it communicated with the unseen world, and propitiated demons, and invoked favors of gods, and reported all manner of glories unknown in the plodding life of the mud hut, the cave, the field or the forest.

But literature did not develop alone. To serve it, since it was something so special and alluring, a particular language began to evolve, a speech more refined than that of quarreling clans and hunting clansmen. And one of the features of this speech was a rhythm that set it off from the uncouth talk of man to man.

But how can we be sure of this? Because of what we know of surviving primitives and their tribal chants. Whether the witch-doctor leads the people in an invocation to the wind-god or the river-god or the sun-god, or whether the head of a family utters an exorcism to drive the ghosts from the hut of a deceased kinsman, or whether the warrior chief joins in a chant to the beloved ancestors for success in battle or the hunt, the outpouring will spontaneously take on a rhythmic swing.

We can see this, for example, in the poetry of the American Indians. Take the Papagos, whose music has been studied in a monograph by Frances Densmore.* For the simplest ceremonies of tribal life, we find the people bursting into song. Opening the pages at random, I find *In the Medicine Man's House,* of which a translation follows:

> To the medicine man's house they have led me,
> To the medicine man's house they have led me,
> Inside the house they have brought me,
> Elder brother is there and feathers fly about,
> The owl feathers sing in the air.

Even in the English rendition, one can detect the rhythmical basis. And this is true also of the other songs, on whose rhythmical aspects Miss Densmore frequently comments.

Another example, from a different volume, should suffice. I quote the beginning of a Shaman's Song of the Kwakiutl of the Pacific Northwest:

> I have been told to heal him, by the good supernatural power.
> I have been told to keep on putting the hemlock ring over him, by the Shaman-of-the-Sea, the good supernatural power.
> I have been told to put back into our friend his soul, by the good supernatural power.
> I have been told to give him long life, by the Long-Life-giver-of-the-Sea, the Chief of High-Water, the good supernatural power.**

The rhythm here is much more evident, along with the literary device of repetition. In this case—and I believe that this is largely true of the songs of uncivilized peoples—the

---

* Frances Densmore, *Papago Music,* Smithsonian Institution, Bureau of American Ethnology, Bulletin 90, Washington, 1929.

** A. Grove Day, *The Sky Clears.* Poetry of the American Indians, New York, 1951.

whole was intended to subserve a magical end, as is to be expected in a society whose institutions are built around magic. But for our purposes the essential fact is that the shaman, together with all other primitive song makers, fell naturally into rhythm, and thus unconsciously, while making some of the world's earliest poetry, showed that rhythm was the foundation of poetic technique.

In various other ways, we can see why this must have been so. Let us imagine, for example, that one of the world's first poets, long before a name for "poet" had been invented, wished to express his feelings for his lady love. Suppose that she impressed him as slender as a bent bow and good to look upon as the full moon. He would utter his thoughts in words, which would not be jerked from him in harsh, discordant phrases, for then he would be jolted and jarred and do violence to the gentleness of his mood. Spontaneously, he would give us the benefit of some tribute such as this:

> O my Love, you are slender as the bow when it bends at the
>   hunting-time,
> And good to look upon as the moon when its face is round
>   just after the time of the setting sun.

Here, presumably, would be no measured lines; but here would be a cadence which was not that of prose. And so here, hallmarked by that very cadence, a pronounced step would have been taken toward a poetic literature. Unconsciously, music would have been recognized as at the basis of poetry.

As poetic utterance became more frequent and tribal bards were admired and praised, a time would arrive when the chants would recite great communal exploits—the downing of a boar, wild bull or mammoth; the gallant duel of two tribesmen; the routing of an enemy people. And story-tellers

would recount these feats over and over again, and hand the
tales down to their sons and their sons' sons; and the rhythmic
form would be found best to give the narratives a ringing utterance; and in time it would be discovered that, in order to be
most effective, rhythm would have to follow a more or less
regular pattern. And thus simple ballads would arise, and men
would tell of love and war somewhat in the manner of the old
anonymous writers of England and Scotland:

> O waly, waly up the bank,
>   And waly, waly down the brae,
> And waly, waly yon burn side,
>   Where I and my love were wont to gae,

and,

> A fair maid sat in her bower door,
>   Wringing her lily hands;
> And by it came a sprightly youth,
>   Fast tripping o'er the strands.
>
> "Where gang ye, young John," she says,
>   "Sae early in the day?
> It gars me think, by your fast trip,
>   Your journey's far away."

Here the rhythm is of the simplest, and permits many
metrical variations. And the meter—consisting of a measured
succession of iambic feet—is at the basis of the music even
more than is the rhyme, and bridges the wide gulf between
the ballad and prose.

The metrical compositions of early peoples, however, are
perhaps on the whole as much concerned with religion as with
story-telling. We see this in India, whose *Rig-veda*—the most
ancient of the Vedas—is composed of 1028 hymns comprising
nearly eleven thousand stanzas by various authors. But though
the writing may have occupied as much as five centuries, even

the earliest of the poems follows a strict metrical scheme, and indicates a long pre-existent tradition of formal composition. Thus the beginnings of established Hindu prosody, and of measured rhythmical utterance, can be dated back well over three thousand years.

Metrical poetry, likewise, reached a considerable development in ancient China, in the *Shi King* or *Classic of Poetry,* which was edited and selected by Confucius five centuries before Christ. And in ancient Babylon, poetry was prominent in the renowned *Izdubar* epic, with its tale of the descent of the goddess of love Isthar into hell, and with religious chants and supplications whose rhythmical element is evident even in translation. I quote three lines:

> O mistress, in the anguish of my heart have I raised cries to thee; declare forgiveness!
> O mistress, to thy servant declare respite! May thy heart be at rest.
> Unto thy servant who hath experienced sorrow, grant mercy.*

In Egypt also, men cried out with a resounding rhythmical utterance on matters of religion and personal emotion. We can see this, for example, in the *Hymn to Usertesan III,* a chant discovered not many years ago near the pyramid of a monarch who may have antedated Christ by as much as thirty centuries. These lines are from the version by Carl Holliday:

> Twice joyous are the gods; thou hast made from their worship!
> Twice joyous are thy children; thou hast made their homeland!

---

* R. F. Harper, *Assyrian and Babylonian Literature,* New York, 1901.

Twice joyous are thy fathers; thou hast added to their
    wealth!
Twice joyous is Egypt in thy strength; thou hast
    maintained her power!
Twice mighty is the monarch of his fortress, more
    than a million warriors!*

Apparently the unknown poet of five millennia ago realized
that, in order to express himself effectively in poetry, he needed
a more or less regular recurrence of syllables beating like waves
against a sea-coast.

In the Egyptian chant, though it long antedated the Old
Testament, we see indications of a literary tradition similar to
that of the inspired passages of the Bible. And we find a
rhythm that brings to mind a celebrated verse such as this
from *Isaiah*:

And he shall judge among the nations, and shall rebuke
many people: and they shall beat their swords into plow-
shares, and their spears into pruninghooks: nation shall not
lift up sword against nation, neither shall they learn war
any more.**

Or take this from *Psalms*:

Then the earth shook and trembled; the foundations also
of the hills moved and were shaken, because he was wroth.

There went up a smoke out of his nostrils, and fire out of
his mouth devoured: coals were kindled by it.

He bowed the heavens also, and came down: and darkness
was under his feet.

And he rode upon a cherub, and did fly: yea, he did fly
upon the wings of the wind.

---

* Carl Holliday, *The Dawn of Literature*, New York, 1931.
** *Isaiah*, 2, iv.

He made darkness his secret place; his pavilion round about him were dark waters and thick clouds of the skies.*

This may, strictly speaking, be what we know as poetic prose, for there is no evidence of a measured meter; yet the rhythm is not only unmistakable, but indispensable in producing an effect above that of prose.

But in the ancient lands of poetry's highest attainment—in classical Greece and Rome—we do not find unmeasured or irregular lines, but poetry rooted in an exacting meter. It was in Greece and Rome that the dactylic hexameter came into flower—the dactylic hexameter, which made possible the swing and power of the *Iliad*, the *Odyssey*, and the *Aeneid*, and which inspired Tennyson to speak of Virgil as "Wielder of the stateliest measure ever moulded by the lips of man." Though it is alien to the English language, something of its expansiveness and glory is evident even in translation. I quote a few typical lines from a recent version of the *Iliad*:

Thus she spake; and she smiled—the ox-eyed, worshipful
    Hera;
Then, with the smoke, she placed in her own fair bosom
    the girdle.
Unto her mansion the daughter of Zeus, Aphrodite,
    departed.
Hera leapt down in haste and left the peak of Olympus,
Passed o'er the land of Pieria and over Emanthia, the
    lovely,
Sped on over the snow-covered hills of the horse-breeding
    Thracians,
Over the topmost peaks, nor grazed the ground with her
    footsteps . . .**

---

* *Psalms*, 18, vii-xi.
** William Benjamin Smith and Walter Miller, *The Iliad of Homer*, a line for line translation in dactylic hexameters, New York, 1944.

It is hard to see how the same effect could arise except through the rush and flow of the long sweeping line. The Greeks and Romans, like all poetic experimenters, came to realize that the continuous effect of similar syllables, beating upon the mind without awkward pauses or dissonances, not only served to convey an impression of beauty, but reinforced the power of the thought, enhanced it with a feeling of grandeur and magnificence, stamped it upon the mind, and made it memorable. Thus great poetry, in ancient times as in all times, had a resemblance to great music; like great music, it could not exist without the underlying and overflowing rhythm; like great music, it spoke with the voice of the on-sweeping wind, the rolling waves, and the tidal ebb and flow within the heart of man. And like great music, it retained an element of song amid all the delicacies, the subtleties and the complexities of utterance.

§ 2

In the poetry of many lands in the thousands of years between the birth of classical antiquity and the dawn of our own day, we can see the same relationship between rhythm, music and poetry. In the comparatively rude work of the Anglo-Saxons, meter is at the basis of a poem such as *Beowulf*—a non-rhyming, alliterative epic in which a musical effect is produced by the two strong accented syllables of each short half line. Much greater refinements of poetry are to be found in Persia, where Omar Khayyam was but a lesser luminary amid the multitudes who broke out in song and satire, epigram and narrative with an artistically controlled rhythm and meter—poets whose very names are mostly unknown in the west, though Firdausi, Khakani, Nizami, Rumi, Sadi, Hafiz and many others have been famed and revered in the land of their birth. Something similar may be said, again, of the Arab world, in which we not only observe rhymed poetry in high esteem and development, but see that regard for rhythm which is universal wherever the name of poetry is honored. Having created an art which they held worthy of preservation, the Arabs were at pains to preserve it, as we may see from the following:

> The various and varied rhythms discovered by unknown Beduins at an unknown date, possibly in the fifth century of our era, conceivably earlier, have not been departed from or significantly added to down to the present time.*

In Europe no less than in the east, as every student of versification knows, rhythm has been the lattice-work of poetry down through the Middle Ages with its songs, ballads and epics, and almost to the threshold of our own generation. The great transformation—for there *has been* a great transformation—did not come with writers such as Coventry Patmore and Matthew Arnold, who experimented with metrical variations without abandoning meter or forsaking rhythm. The great transformation may be said to date from Whitman, who, however, would have been the first to deny a departure from the laws of rhythm; he was merely, or so he supposed, submitting rhythm to the discipline of his own perceptions. This fact is attested by much internal evidence: take, for example, the line "When lilacs last in the dooryard bloom'd," and invert one word so as to substitute "When lilacs in the dooryard last bloomed." The meaning remains unchanged, but in all other essentials the line has been destroyed—and destroyed because the rhythm has been ruined. This may indeed indicate that, in his free rhythms, Whitman had a certain success, but alas! the success was too limited, he yielded too frequently to the temptation to follow the rhythms of prose, and the precedent was bequeathed to the next generation, until our own

---

* A. J. Arberry, in the Introduction to *Moorish Poetry*, a translation of "The Pennants," an Anthology compiled in 1243 by the Andalusian Ibn Sa'id, Cambridge, Eng., 1953.

day is the stage for such confusion that many readers and writers actually do not know what constitutes the rhythm of prose, and what the rhythm of poetry. And the result has been that our typical so-called poetry has abounded in lines such as these:

> This building is unequalled for expense and size,
> These doors, constructed to heroic scale,
> Suitable to the huge dimension of
> Science in the modern enterprise,
> Will close at five . . .
>
> (Edith Henrich)

> Thought is false happiness: the idea
> That merely by thinking one can,
> Or may, penetrate, not may,
> But can, that one is sure, to be able . . .
>
> (Wallace Stevens)

> About suffering they were never wrong,
> The Old Masters: how well they understood
> Its human position; how it takes place
> While someone else is eating or opening a window
>   or just walking dully along . . .
>
> (W. H. Auden)

> Madame Sosostris, famous clairvoyante,
> Had a bad cold, nevertheless
> Is known to be the wisest woman in Europe
> With a wicked pack of cards.
>
> (T. S. Eliot)

It strikes me that work such as this—and this is not exceptionally bad, merely characteristic—is most curious from the point of view of rhythm, after the centuries in which the poets of the west and of the east have developed poetry as a thing rhythmically apart, rhythmically above prose, rhythmically capable of wonder-working. To show that most so-called

modern rhythms are in no way poetic, and differ in no ob-
servable respect from the rhythms of ordinary prose, one need
merely strip a passage of the disguise of its line divisions. The
above excerpt from *The Waste Land* then reads as follows:

>   Madame Sosostris, famous clairvoyante, had a bad cold,
> nevertheless is known to be the wisest woman in Europe,
> with a wicked pack of cards.

Would you recognize anything poetic about this? Would
you detect a poetic rhythm? I confess that I would not. Yet
I fear that, were I a young poet, with teachers that lauded this
work as representative of the best in poetry, I would be confused—deeply, darkly confused. I might not be sure which
way to turn. Not knowing much if anything of the poets that
have glorified the literature of many lands, I might question
if there really was such a thing as a resounding, an enchanting
rhythm. I might wonder if rhythm actually had any value.
And I might ask myself if good prose is not really superior to
poetry, since in most distinguished prose I could find a swing,
an uplift, a nobility unapproached in the commonplace, nearly
rhythmless lines recommended as typical of our poetic best.

Because unknown numbers of poets today are in just this
state of mind, and are being led either toward poetic sterility
or toward prose, let me try to indicate just what our poetry
might have been if the giants of the past had not, first of all,
followed the general laws of rhythm, and, beyond that, paid
allegiance to the prescriptions of meter.

§ 3

Let us begin with the acknowledged leader among all who
have ever used the English tongue. With apologies to Shakespeare, I will start by quoting the opening of one of his best-
known sonnets, then will reproduce the passage as it might

have been written had the poet wished to escape the so-called bondage of meter. Here are the actual lines:

> Shall I compare thee to a summer's day?
> Thou art more lovely and more temperate.

And here is how they might have been composed, with two metrical variations, though with no change in the figures or meanings:

> Shall I liken thee to a summer's day?
> Thou art more lovely and temperate.

"Liken" is not greatly inferior to "compare," and conveys the same thought; the omitted second "more" served no purpose except of rhetoric and meter. Yet what has happened to the passage? It has been blasted apart. It is no longer poetry; it is limping prose, whose halting rhythms do not reinforce the thought or make it impressive. In this form it would not have outlasted the centuries; it would have been unlikely to outlast a first reading. Yet the difference between the two passages, remember, is mainly metrical.

Now consider an example from one of the Shakespearian songs:

> Take, O take those lips away
>   That so sweetly were forsworn;
> And those eyes, the break of day,
>   Lights that do mislead the morn ...

Suppose that we dismember the meter:

> Take, take those lips away,
>   That have been so sweetly forsworn,
> Also those eyes, the break of day,
>   Lights misleading the morn.

Anyone with the slightest poetic sense would instantly recognize the first passage as delightfully lyrical. But anyone coming upon the second version for the first time would have the sense of something wrong. The difference between the two stanzas, however, is not one of meaning, but of song. Shakespeare's lines sing; my own corrupted lines do not sing. And this is because Shakespeare has followed his own rhythmic sense and the laws of meter; whereas my version is written in deliberate violation of rhythm and meter.

As a final illustration from Shakespeare, let us take a passage of blank verse. Here are the majestic opening lines of Richard the Third:

> Now is the winter of our discontent
> Made glorious summer by this sun of York;
> And all the clouds that loured upon our house
> In the deep bosom of the ocean buried.

With a view to thought only and in disregard of meter, this might be rendered as follows:

> Now is our winter of discontent
> Made glorious summer by this York's sun;
> And the clouds that lour'd upon our house
> All buried in the deep ocean's bosom.

It is safe to say that no actor could effectively recite the altered version. Nor could any reader be stirred by it. Yet again the difference is not one of content, but of rhythm. We should note, however, that Shakespeare has permitted himself some variations from strict metrical regularity, particularly in the fourth line; such variations, skillfully controlled, may actually improve the rhythmical effect, and are in fact indispensable in avoiding monotony. But they must be controlled by a well-attuned ear so as not to destroy the metrical pattern;

Shakespeare in this case, for example, permits himself no departure from the iambic norm. Only because he adheres to that norm, with legitimate variations, has he won his way across the generations as a master of blank verse.

Precisely the same may be said of another master, Milton. Here are five lines from *Paradise Lost*:

> Join voices, all ye living souls, ye birds,
> That, singing, up to heaven-gate ascend,
> Bear on your wings and in your notes His praise.
> Ye that in waters glide, and ye that walk
> The earth, and stately tread, or lowly creep ...

The words "stately tread" truly express these lines; surely, no reader can be quite insensitive to the stately tread. But what becomes of the stateliness if we alter the lines, though again without doing violence to the thought?

> Join voices, ye living souls, ye birds,
> That, singing, ascend up to heaven-gate,
> Bear His praise on your wings and notes,
> Ye that glide in waters, and walk
> The earth, and tread stately, or creep lowly ...

This, I submit, is nearer to what might be expected of a typical poet of today. But this, being without the metrical base and so without the rhythm of the original, brings us none of the epic suggestions of Milton; this is flat and unmemorable.

And if such ruin can be worked in blank verse merely by tampering with the meter, think of what a similar tampering would do to the great mass of our lyrical poetry. Burns and Wordsworth and Shelley, Keats and Byron and Tennyson, Moore and Coleridge and the Rossettis and Swinburne and a host of others whose voices are those of song and whose effects often depend upon the turn of a phrase, simply could not exist without their underlying rhythms; like a house whose foundations have been blown from under it, they would collapse.

But nothing like this can be said of our so-called modernists. Just for the sake of comparison, let us note what happens when we take deliberate liberties with their rhythms. I pull a book from the shelves; it happens to be T. S. Eliot's *Four Quartets*. And the piece at which I open is *East Coker*, which commences as follows:

> In my beginning is my end. In succession
> Houses rise and fall, crumble, are extended,
> Are removed, destroyed, restored, or in their place
> Is an open field, or a factory, or a by-pass.

Let me change this, as I have changed passages by greater poets. Once more I do not interfere with the meaning:

> In my beginning my end is. In succession
> Houses fall and rise, houses crumble, are extended,
> Are removed, restored, destroyed, or else in their place
> There is an open field, a by-pass, or a factory.

Aside from adding one or two superfluous words, removing an "or," and transposing the order of certain other words, I have not really done much to this passage. Rhythmically the second version is not noticeably inferior to the first; hence its total effect is not much inferior. And the reason is obvious: the passage had no metrical or rhythmical basis to begin with, unless one regard it as extremely defective blank verse— and what does not exist cannot be destroyed. Actually, as anyone can prove if he takes the trouble to write it out without the division into lines, Eliot's work is no more than prose, and ordinary prose at that; therefore its rhythms, unlike those of Shakespeare and Milton, produce little effect upon the reader's mind, and so can be shifted almost at will with no great likelihood of loss. It is only when a rhythm has been forged with artistic skill and precision that it cannot be altered without disaster.

None of this, of course, should be taken to mean that the poet should be cramped in his choice of meters; after all, meter means nothing more nor less than the division of poetry into lines of a specified number of a particular kind of feet, which in turn may be combined into stanzaic systems. And such stanzaic systems offer opportunities for almost unlimited diversity, and may enable new patterns to be found even now by experimenting poets—and by "experimenting" I do not mean "experimental" in the sense of throwing overboard all that we have ever learned, but rather in the sense of building upon yesterday's discoveries in the effort to reach new heights tomorrow.

But may the poet never abandon meter in favor of rhythms of his own choice? Let us consider the experience of the past. Strict regularity actually has been abandoned, and abandoned with notable success in rhymed poems such as Arnold's *The Forsaken Merman* and Browning's *Home Thoughts from Abroad*, and in a whole class of compositions with the same general technical features as the above: the irregular ode. We can all mention some famous examples: Milton's *Lycidas*, though this is technically an elegy, and though the irregularity is not pronounced; the odes of Dryden; Lowell's *Commemoration Ode*, unbeloved of schoolboys; Keats' *Ode to Psyche*; and Wordsworth's *Ode on Intimations of Immortality*, whose opening lines show the irregular ode at its typical best:

> There was a time when meadow, grove, and stream,
> The earth, and every common sight,
> To me did seem
> Apparell'd in celestial light,
> The glory and the freshness of a dream,

It is not now as it hath been of yore;—
   Turn whereso'er I may,
      By night or day,
The things which I have seen I now can see no more.

Here the structural features are self-evident: the lines are rhymed, they follow an iambic norm, they vary from two to six feet, and the different lengths are mingled at the poet's discretion. Yet the result is entirely agreeable to the ear and mind; the result does no violence to the natural relationship between poetry and music.

It is curious that, so long as poets cling to rhyme, they are not infrequently successful with variations such as those of the irregular ode. But as soon as they abandon rhyme, they seem to lose an essential guide; rhythmically they surrender their grip. We may indeed note a few exceptions, such as Whitman's exquisite lines beginning, "At the last, tenderly," and certain compositions of Kahlil Gibran, which are so near the borderline of prose and poetry that we may regard them either as poetry or as poetic prose. Take these lines from *The Garden of the Prophet*:

O Mist, my sister, white breath not yet held in a mould,
I return to you, a breath white and voiceless,
A word not yet uttered. . . .

O Mist, my sister, I come back, a heart listening in his
   depths,
Even as your heart,
A desire throbbing and aimless even as your desire,
A thought not yet gathered, even as your thought.

Personally, I would not quibble as to the designation. Whether poetry or prose, this is beautiful writing; this has not only the sense and suggestions of poetry, but a rhythm which is gratefully received by the ear, and upon which the whole largely depends for its effects. But how often do our so-called free poets reach this level? The answer is: practically never. On the contrary, they descend to the type of writing I quoted a few pages back—descend to verses that could be printed with impunity in the form of prose, since no one would ever suspect that they were not prose. Probably not a poet in a thousand is without need of a trellis around which to wind his rhythms; and any such trellis can be powerfully bolstered by rhyme, and falls to pieces in the absence of a specific type of recurring prosodic foot. It is apparently for this reason that meter in some form has been part of the basic structure of poetry in most lands, from ancient Greece and Rome to medieval Arabia and Persia, and from China and Japan to the countries of modern Europe. And it is for this reason that any poet who forsakes meter does so at his peril, and is far more likely than not to end on the desert plains of drabbest prose.

III

"Should I Employ Rhyme?"

Considered from the abstract point of view, one of the most curious of literary tools is rhyme. It is a mere musical device, often pleasing, sometimes even entrancing; it has no necessary relation to meaning, yet may control meaning by governing the turn of a phrase. And despite this apparent contradiction, it has become one of the outstanding elements in western prosody. Without it, the greater part of English poetry as we know it, would be unthinkable. From the *Canterbury Tales* to the sonnets of Keats, from the didacticism of Pope to the lyricism of Poe, from the songs of Lovelace and Herrick to the metrical fluencies of O'Shaughnessy and Swinburne, rhyme has played a major if not an indispensable role. Can one even imagine what would happen to a passage such as, for example, "Bards of passion and of mirth / Ye have left your souls on earth," if rhyme were to be eliminated?

Yet rhyme was virtually unknown in the ancient world. In India it is foreign to the great body of classical poetry, although it was a feature of the lyrics of the Bengalese writer Jayadeva (twelfth century). In the west, it is believed to have originated in the Latin verse of the ecclesiastics of the age of Tertullian; in any case, it is known that rhymed sacred poetry had come into being by the fourth century—perhaps as a device to aid in the memorizing and singing of long religious pieces. But whatever the source, the new tool of poets grew into rapid and general use; it rose to be characteristic of the verse of the Middle Ages; it became conspicuous in poet-haunted Persia and Arabia; after the fourteenth century, it dominated all Europe, except for Spain, where assonance remained popular; and until the iconoclastic and often anarchic movements of the twentieth century, it has been undisputed master throughout the Continent and England, despite the efforts made now and then by poets such as Campion, Carducci, William Collins and Heine to escape at least in part from its shackles.

When a device has won enthusiasm from so many poets and enraptured so many audiences in so many lands for so many centuries, there is more than a presumption that it has rare and high merits. Let us inquire, therefore, as to just what rhyme does to poetry.

Some of its advantages, of course, are self-evident. We know that the commonest jingle could not exist without rhyme; without rhyme, the thought of the commonest jingle would be much harder to remember. Let us take two not especially distinguished lines by Charles Lamb:

> I saw where in the shroud did lurk
> A curious frame of Nature's work.

These lines can be recalled without much effort; and being recalled, they force their meaning home. But suppose that Lamb had written:

> I saw where in the shroud did lurk
> A curious frame of nature's toil.

The difference between the two passages is not merely that the first has more of a savor. A sharper distinction is that the second is much harder to fix in mind.

Now consider another example. Here are the opening lines of Charles Wolfe's simple but feeling lyric *To Mary*:

> If I had thought thou couldst have died,
>   I might not weep for thee;
> But I forgot, when by thy side,
>   That thou couldst mortal be.

Note the effect if Wolfe had written:

> If I had thought thou couldst have died,
>   I might not weep for thee.
> But I forgot, when near at hand,
>   That thou wert mortal flesh.

Somehow, while the original evokes sympathy, the rhyme-less paraphrase leaves one cold; it is a mere tasteless broth. And this should emphasize a second fact about rhyme: it not only accentuates thought, it accentuates emotion, and indeed often aids to produce emotional effects impossible without it.

Let us glance at a further case: the last stanza of Swinburne's *The Garden of Proserpine*:

> Then star nor sun shall waken,
>   Nor any change of light;
> Nor sound of waters shaken,
>   Nor any sound or sight;
> Nor wintry leaves nor vernal,
> Nor days nor things diurnal:
> Only the sleep eternal
>   In an eternal night.

The rhyme here is almost the poem; it is impossible to imagine the passage without rhyme; any attempted rhymeless reproduction would be but the shadow of the original. Strangely, Swinburne's rhyme is so important in bringing home the thought that it seems a part of the thought.

In epigrammatic work, something similar is true; there is no other epigram with quite the brilliance or the barb of a rhymed one, nor any that can impress us with quite the same wonder, joy or melancholy. This time I turn to ancient Greece, to Strabo's quatrain To Producè, as translated by J. M. Edmonds:

> Come let us bathe, and flow'rs for chaplets twine,
> Then fill great cuffs and quaff unwater'd wine:

> Brief is our life of joyance; soon, sweet friend,
> Old Age will come to thwart and Death to end.

The quatrain says as much in the following form:

> Come let us bathe, and flow'rs for chaplets weave,
> Then fill great cuffs and quaff unwater'd wine:
> Brief is our life of joyance; soon, sweet friend,
> Old Age will come to thwart and Death to close.

Yes, the second version says as much, but somehow does not *seem* to say as much; the point has been shorn from the rapier. The question here is not, as in the case of *The Garden of Proserpine,* concerned with the poem's whole atmosphere and beauty; the question is mainly that of the incisiveness of the message. And if the message has more of a cutting edge when rhyme is present, why should the poet deny himself that moving power?

The same may be said even more emphatically of light verse, in which rhyme is often half the fun. Strange and outlandish rhymes, of a sort impossible in serious poetry, may give humorous verse a peculiar zest and flavor; and these rhymes are often polysyllabic, as in "perpendicular," and "vehicular," "ornamental" and "transcendental," "Napoleon" and "aeolian," and even a combination so silly-sounding as "Socrates" and "socks and cheese." It does not even matter if the rhyme is obviously made to order, as in the beginning of Thomas Hood's *Tale of a Trumpet*:

> Of all old women hard of hearing
> The deafest, sure, was Dame Eleanor Spearing!

We know, of course, that if the lady were hard of seeing, she would be Dame Eleanor Speeing, but that does not at all interfere with our enjoyment. Consider, by contrast, how uninteresting she would be if "Of all old women hard of hearing / The deafest, sure, was Dame Eleanor Curtis!"

The use of rare and fantastic rhymes for comic purposes has been well illustrated by W. S. Gilbert. Thus, in one of his Colonel's songs in *Patience*, he rhymes "quackery" and "Thackeray," "Peverill" and "Sacheverell," and "Defoe" and "Guizot," and proceeds to the following:

> If you want a receipt for this soldierlike paragon
>   Get at the wealth of the Czar (if you can)—
> The family pride of a Spaniard from Aragon—
>   Force of Mephisto pronouncing a ban—
> A smack of Lord Weatherford, reckless and rollicky—
>   Swagger of Roderick, heading his clan—
> The keen penetration of Paddington Pollaky—
>   Grace of an Odalisque on a divan,
> The genius strategic of Caesar or Hannibal—
>   Skill of Sir Garnet in thrashing a cannibal . . .

After Hannibal, it is true, the cannibal was almost inevitable, since there is no other rhyme. But this hardly detracts from the rollicking effects of the several-syllabled rhymes and galloping meter.

In contrast to the extravagance of the above, excellent comic effects are sometimes obtained by a restrained use of rhyme. Take Cowper's humorous ballad *John Gilpin*, with typical stanzas such as,

> Said John, "It is my wedding day,
>   And all the world would stare
> If wife should dine at Edmonton
>   And I should dine at Ware."

The matter-of-fact quality of this, aided by the matter-of-fact rhyme, adds to the comical effect.

§ 2

A further purpose of rhyme is its function of binding lines together so as to form definite stanzaic patterns. True, such patterns are possible in exceptional cases even without rhyme; in the Sapphics used by Swinburne and others, we have unrhymed four-line stanzas whose effects depend largely upon the grace of the feminine endings. In Tennyson's *Tears, Idle Tears* and in his lines beginning "Now sleeps the crimson petal, now the white," we have effective unrhymed stanzas; but in both cases there is really a skillful adaptation of blank verse, aided by carefully contrived repetitions of phrases. In Collins' *Ode to Evening* we find another adaptation of blank verse, in which two five-foot lines are followed by two three-foot lines to form an unrhymed stanza, which, however, has not evoked sufficient admiration to have had many imitators. And an occasional recent poet has, with some measure of success, given us an unrhymed lyric with a stanzaic pattern. But such cases have been few and far between, and have had little if any influence on poetry as a whole.

The fact remains that without rhyme we could not have had such important structures as the Spenserian stanza, the *rime royal*, the heroic couplet, the traditional four-foot, three-foot ballad form, most of the better known lyrical forms, the various French forms (except possibly the sestina), and last, but far from least, the sonnet. True, there have been some claims of rhymeless sonnets—which should be taken about as seriously as claims of paintings without shades or colors, dances without movement, or piano sonatas without a piano. Even if good fourteen-line unrhymed poems are possible, such poems do not and cannot have the specific qualities of the sonnet, since they lack the sonnet's specific means of obtaining its effects. And those means, both in the Italian form and in the Shakespearian, are connected with rhyme. Consider the beginning of one of Rossetti's sonnets:

> When vain desire at last and vain regret
> Go hand in hand to death, and all in vain,

> What shall assuage the unforgotten pain
> And teach the unforgetful to forget?

Here, obviously, the poetry is quite as much in the wording as in the meaning. And an essential part of the wording is the rhyme. Without the rhyme, the thought might still be there, but it could not be expressed with quite the same compelling smoothness, nor would it strike with the characteristic impact of the sonnet. It might, indeed, have the impact of blank verse, but that is something different; it is something that experience has proved best on the whole in longer pieces; its inappropriateness for the more concise, more emotional utterance is indicated by the fact that the greatest masters of blank verse, Shakespeare and Milton, turned to the sonnet for the utterance of their personal sentiments. Nor did they try to produce rhymeless sonnets!

§ 3

"But this," the reader may argue, "is only telling half the story. You have mentioned the advantages of rhyme, but said nothing of its disadvantages."

"Very well then," I may answer. "What *are* its disadvantages?"

"Well, first of all," the reader may continue, "there is the difficulty of rhyme. And the fact that it is an impediment in the way of free expression."

Let us therefore consider these contentions. *Is* rhyme difficult? *Is* it an impediment in the way of free expression? The answer must necessarily vary with the individual. First of all, it is obvious that rhyme has not imposed such an interference as to prevent a host of English poets from creating, in rhyme, a great mass of some of the world's most accomplished poetry. As for the difficulty—all art is difficult; no stroke of the chisel can be made without strain and effort; the road to attainment in art is precisely the road to the mastery of difficulties. This does not mean that impediments should be imposed merely for the sake of surmounting them; but likewise it does not mean that difficulties should be avoided just because they demand thought or exertion. If what is desired is a lazy man's paradise, why seek to create art, why write poetry at all?

The truth, however, is that the difficulties of rhyme have been exaggerated. The usual experience of those who have done much verse-writing has, I believe, been that rhymes come easily, often with little or no struggle, sometimes so facilely that they seem fairly to leap out on each other's heels. As one not without practice in this field, I can say that rhyme has never really hindered anything I have wanted to say; the resources of language, the variety of words and the possible turns of phrasing are so extensive that even a moderate ingenuity is ordinarily able to surmount all obstacles. And I have no reason to doubt that what is true in my case applies also in most others. I will go beyond that and say that rhyme is often a positive help, by throwing out suggestions—suggestions of the most effective turns of phrase by which to convey one's thought. Strangely, the poet sometimes attains an impression of inevitability by the very act of picking the appropriate rhyme.

Observe, as an example, the opening stanza of O'Shaughnessy's delicate *Ode*:

> We are the music-makers,
>   And we are the dreamers of dreams,
> Wandering by lone sea-breakers,
>   And sitting by desolate streams;
> World-losers and world-forsakers,
>   On whom the pale moon gleams:
> Yet we are the movers and shakers
>   Of the world for ever, it seems.

I have not, naturally, had any personal information from the author; nor have I read any statement as to how he came to write this poem. But from what I know of poets and poetry-making, several facts seem reasonably clear. The first is that the author's original thought is the one expressed in the opening two lines. And the second conclusion is that, having ended these lines with "makers" and "dreams," he looked about him for suitable rhymes, and chose "breakers," "forsakers," and "shakers," "streams," "gleams," and "seems," because these happened to suit his purposes. Yet those words did more than to rhyme; they harmonized with his thought and enhanced its expression, so that now we can hardly imagine the stanza in any other form. To find just the right rhyming words may, indeed, have been difficult, just as it is difficult to find the right non-rhyming words. But what of that? The reward of an enchanting lyric should be sufficient repayment. And the lyric is what it is—one of the most memorable in the language —not only for what it says, and not only for the way in which it rhymes, but because what it says is furthered by the way in which it rhymes.

Are there any additional objections to rhyme? "Ah, yes," says the reader, "there is a most important one. Rhymes tend to be overused, obvious and trite; the same rhymes are likely to be repeated *ad infinitum*, if not *ad nauseam*, with the result that the effect of freshness is lost."

Every poetry lover knows, of course, that there is a measure of truth in this claim. If one reads the word "strife," one does not like to feel that, as inevitably as the sound of the hammer follows the pounding of the nail, this word will be rhymed with "life." And the same may be said of a few other combinations, such as "love" and "dove," "high" and "sky," "breeze" and "trees," etc. But every good poet recognizes these overworked combinations, and avoids them whenever possible; if he feels it necessary to use them, he usually does so in triple or quadruple rhymes or spaces them several lines apart, so that they may be less obvious. But the number of such well-known combinations, in which the reader can almost guess the rhyme, are relatively few. In more cases than not, so many rhyming words are possible that one would almost have to be clairvoyant in order to know what to expect. How many rhymes are there for "lore"? Or for "lair"? Or for "lie"? Or for "lay"? So many, certainly, that it is usually out of the question to foresee a particular choice.

And what if a poet does rhyme "lore" with "more," and this has been done by others? Unless he is attempting a mere *tour de force* or a rollicking light verse, he does not seek his originality in his rhymes. And what, after all, is the purpose of rhyme? To show the poet's verbal dexterity in the game of picking rarely used or never-used words? Or to produce an effect upon the reader? If the poet's aim is the latter, all that counts is how the reader reacts to the rhymes. And I think it may be stated unequivocally that the reader reacts pleasantly to any rhymes that seem to give a natural effect, which means that one should pick an obvious rhyme between "light" and "night" that carries out the meaning, rather than a far-from-obvious "light" and "recondite" that does violence to the meaning, or appears strained or forced.

The reader's tolerance in this respect, I submit, will be found to be greater than the average critic's. If we leave out of account a few rhymes of the "love-dove" variety, which have made themselves suspect through repetition, I do not believe that the poet will ever lose in the respect of his audience by employing whatever rhyme seems best suited to his thought. After all, no reader's head is a compendium of all the rhymes ever used; no reader asks if a particular rhyme has ever been chosen by Ben Jonson, or Donne, or Blake, or

Southey or any one of a thousand other poets. All that the reader is interested to know—and usually even this knowledge will be merely subconscious—is whether the rhyme fulfills its purpose: whether it fits into the musical scheme, and helps to carry out the thought. And if this is all that interests the reader, it is all that need concern the poet.

IV

The Use and Misuse of Words

Whether you express yourself orally or in writing, whether you produce a letter, an epic, an oration, a news report, or a business suggestion, your building blocks are words, and nothing but words. And if this is true of prose, it is even more sharply true of poetry, which has a compression and a precision beyond that of prose, and in which the choice of a word may consequently count for much more. This has been recognized by all the earlier writers on poetry; and as a result, in all periods before our own, the relation of the poet to his words has been fairly well defined: he must pick those words that express his meaning most fully and clearly, those that frame it most incisively, most vividly, picturesquely or suggestively, so that his verses may shine in their most becoming setting. The room for individual choice has been, obviously, unending: Milton was free to refer to "Nut-brown ale," and Cowper to locks "once auburn-bright," and Gray to "Helicon's harmonious spring," and Wordsworth to a womanly "phantom of delight," and there was none to challenge the expression or to ask whether anything like it had ever been used before.

But the glorious age of freedom, in which there was no test but the judgment of the poet and the appropriateness of his choice, has paradoxically been ended by the era of emancipation. In contrast to his unshackled predecessor, the poet of today is worried by the plethora of rules laid down by the officials of the New Liberty. And those rules, reasonable in certain respects, are fantastic in others; if generally obeyed, they would give verse-writing some resemblance to a handicap race, and leave the poet so cramped by self-restrictions that he could barely hobble.

First of all, there is the preoccupation with the trite, the cliché. If I wished to be facetious, I might say that the tritest thing in the world is the outcry against triteness. But just what do we mean by "trite"? The Standard Dictionary defines it as "Used so often as to be hackneyed; made commonplace by frequent repetition." And this definition may serve as well as any. We will agree, of course, that it is undesirable for poets to use words or expressions "made commonplace by frequent repetition"—that is, if there is some uncommonplace substitute. But as a matter of fact, there is not always such a substitute.

We should distinguish, I believe, between expressions which are contrived by particular poets and would not naturally occur to many persons, and expressions which are so much a part of the order of things that they cannot help occurring to anyone, and have no exact replacements. For example, when Coleridge refers to "the ribb'd sea-sand," he presents an original, an exact, and a striking picture; but if other poets also referred to "the ribb'd sea-sand," they would pass the limits of due liberty; the phrase was contrived by Coleridge, and cannot be often repeated without becoming over-used and imitative, and therefore trite and commonplace. The same, similarly, applies when Keats offers us something so original as "O soft embalmer of the still midnight!", or when Shelley speaks of the dead leaves driven "like ghosts from an enchanter fleeing"—these phrases, striking as they are upon first use, would become overworked and consequently trite if repeated.

But a different law applies to a phrase which is generic and therefore not contrived. Any child may and does mention "blue skies" and "green trees," for the word-combinations are both simple and natural, and express a relationship which everyone, except perhaps the color-blind, will admit to exist, and which, besides, cannot be exactly defined in any other words. Therefore the expressions "blue skies" and "green trees," though they contain no originality and pretend to no originality, can never become really trite. For they do convey meaning; they do call attention to certain everlasting truths, and so are as fresh now as in the infancy of the race. Whether their use is desirable in a particular poem is another matter, but if they are to be excluded it must be on other grounds than of triteness.

Our advanced critics, however, have decreed that "blue skies" and "green trees" are trite, and, being trite, are tabu. And so the poet is obliged to find other words—which might be truly advantageous if any other words were appropriate and revealing. But what other words are possible? "Azure" or "cerulean" skies would actually be trite in a way that "blue skies" are not, and the same is true of "jade" or "emerald" trees. True, one might refer to "lilac" or "heliotrope" skies, and these phrases would not be trite—not at first—though they might be no more accurate than equally untrite "alabaster" or "platinum" trees. We see here the danger: in trying to avoid the cliché, we run headon into absurdity, and this is precisely what many moderns have done, as in E. E. Cummings' "the flyspecked abdominous female," which is hardly the more poetic because not trite; or William Empson's "this civilizing love of death"; or Kenneth Patchen's "blue-assed water"; or Alun Lewis' "mole-blue indolence" of the sun; or Dylan Thomas' "imagining of tumbled mantime," and "Savors the lick of the times through a deadly wood of hair." In these cases and thousands of others, the writer has avoided the trite by the simple method of parting company with the true, the unaffected and the natural.

Let us not forget, moreover, that amid all this chattering about triteness, skies continue to be blue, and trees to be green.

§ 2

But the clamor against triteness does not limit itself to attacks upon adjectives such as "blue" and "green." Under some critics, such as John Ciardi, poetry editor of *The Saturday Review*, the anti-triteness campaign has declared war upon all adjectives. Here, truly, is a major remedy for a minor disease! Because adjectives are sometimes overworked, because they may be used unnecessarily or inappropriately, away with them to the executioner's block! It is a little as if a physician, finding a patient awkward in the use of his fingers, were to order his hands cut off. After all, adjectives, like hands, do have a purpose; they were given to the language because nouns, no matter how abundant and descriptive, are not abundant or descriptive enough to cover the innumerable shades and ramifications of meaning. A "white elephant," obviously, is not necessarily quite the same as "an elephant"; nor are either necessarily equivalent to an "extinct elephant"; nor is an Indian elephant zoologically or otherwise identical with an "African elephant"; nor is it proper to confuse "half-grown elephants" and "adult elephants," or "bull elephants" and "cow elephants," or "rogue elephants" and "tractable elephants," and so on and on indefinitely. Without adjectives, the rose would no longer be red or sweet or thorny, nor would days be wet or shining or foggy, nor would men or women be kind or bold or strong, energetic or resolute or sympathetic. And between John and Jim and Jack and Joe, as between Mary and Martha and Miriam and Mathilda, there would be no distinction whatever.

Even to mention such facts is to dispose of the absurdity of abolishing adjectives. But let us go a step further. Let us admit that, if it is desirable to eliminate adjectives now, it must always have been desirable to eliminate them; which means that all the poets who have lived in subjugation to this superfluous part of speech have been sadly misled, and would have benefited by striking out the unnecessary words.

Let us, therefore, in one or two illustrative cases, observe the advantages of the reform. And let us begin with the opening lines of one of Shakespeare's most quoted sonnets:

> When to the sessions of sweet silent thought
> I summon up remembrance of things past,
> I sigh the lack of many a thing I sought,
> And with old woes new wail my dear time's waste.

The bard of Avon, if modern critics are right, went wretchedly astray here, for he has committed no less than six adjectives in four lines. We shall accordingly transcribe the lines without the offending parts of speech:

> When to the sessions of thought
> I summon up remembrance of things,
> I sigh the lack of things I sought,
> And with woes new wail my time's waste.

Doubtless this is still defective from the advanced point of view, for it uses "new" as an adverb, which should also logically be deleted.

Is another illustration necessary? Then take this from Shelley:

> And, like a dying lady lean and pale,
> Who tottered forth, wrapp'd in a gauzy veil,
> Out of her chamber, led by the insane
> And feeble wanderings of her faded brain,
> The moon arose up in the murky east
> A white and shapeless mass.

Shelley here, if we are to accept the modern position, descends even further than does Shakespeare. There is not a line in which he does not use at least one adjective, and in the opening line he perpetrates no less than three. Suppose, therefore, that we free him of these impediments, and replace his misbegotten passage with an improved version:

> And, like a lady
> Who totters forth, wrapp'd in a veil
> Out of her chamber, led by the
> Wanderings of her brain,
> The moon arose up in the east,
> A mass.

Let those who prefer this rendition step forward and say so!

§ 3

Adjectives (along with adverbs) are of course not the only targets of the modern tilters against the parts of speech. If anything, their enmity against certain nouns is greater still. Their thrusts are aimed especially against the words that denote abstract qualities, such as "truth," "beauty," "soul," etc. We have reached such a state, for example, that "virtue" is considered almost a naughty word, not to be uttered in good poetic company. "Horror" is much more in fashion than "honor," and "grimness" than "goodness"; you may speak of the gross and the vile, but to refer to the "right" is to show yourself behind the times. Curious, is it not, that precisely the words that indicate an uplift in man's spirit, precisely the words that beckon toward the peaks and the stars, are branded as *trite* and hence *tabu*, whereas those that point to the mud and the dust have somehow escaped the corrosion of overuse!

Are we not here witnessing something quite apart from literary criticism? Is it not that the critics are trying to combine poetic prescriptions with their own philosophy, their own skeptical or nihilistic views? Are they not actually without belief in truth, beauty, goodness, soul, etc., and for this reason eager to outlaw the very mention of these things? If so, they are no more justified than a Republican would be in trying to forbid all mention of Democrats, a Communist in trying to prohibit all reference to Capitalists, or an atheist in crying *Verboten* to the use of the name of God. After all, personal beliefs on unrelated subjects should not influence poetic criticism. But we have reason to suppose that personal beliefs have been uppermost—and this may explain a series of dogmatic pronouncements more restrictive of true freedom in poetry than the utmost rigors of meter or rhyme.

In the case of nouns such as "truth" and "beauty" no less than of adjectives and adverbs, there is only one rule that is not pedantic and needlessly restraining. And that rule is that the poet should use any word which the language provides, so long as it seems to further his purpose—so long as it appears likely to produce the best effect upon the reader, who after all is the person to be considered first. Words should, of course, as in all writing, be applied with the greatest economy possible; they should not be redundant or repetitious, unless for the sake of emphasis or effect; they should, in the interest of naturalness, not be obsolete, and not be archaic unless for some special reason; they should be as simple and smooth-sounding and as sharply etched as the circumstances permit, but above all they should aim to convey the particular mood, thought or impression within the author's mind. The poet's time should therefore be devoted to picking the right word as dictated by his own sense of fitness, rather than as determined by arbitrary fiats from above.

Let us take a single example—one which will indicate the natural difficulties in the use of words. Suppose that the poet glances at a stream, and wishes to describe its particular shade. He knows it to be brown, but the word "brown" is too general to convey exactly what he sees. He thinks of "muddy brown," but this gives an unpleasant impression which does not quite fit his mood. He next thinks of "chocolate brown," but so many streams have been chocolate brown that this will not strike a sharp enough note. He then considers "coffee brown"—but wonders if the word "coffee" suggests the color of the bean, or of the undiluted beverage, or of the beverage tempered with milk. No, this expression is too indefinite. The same, he decides, is true of "bark brown" and "root brown," for various barks and roots are of different shades. "Dead-grass brown" gives too light and tawny an impression, and "dead-leaf brown" is too indefinite. Finally he thinks of the brown of particular leaves; dismisses one after another as off color; and ends by deciding that "dead oak-leaf brown" says about what he wants to say. But even now he has not reached his goal, for the phrase is awkward; and it may be long before he has fitted it into his verse.

Thus we will see that there are difficulties enough in the poet's choice of words without new authoritarian restrictions.

V

Keeping Your Windows Clean

In certain poetic quarters nowadays there seems to be a preference for dirty windows. The more shadowed they are by soot and dust, the better liked; and anyone suggesting a scouring rag and soap would be denounced as a heretic. For dirty windows, as even the least observant will agree, provide a barrier between the author and such readers as may wish to look in at him. They make it difficult if not impossible for outsiders to see into a poem and discover the meaning, if any; they even make it possible for poems to be without meaning, or at least without meaning visible to anyone but the author. Besides, they give an impression of profundity, according to the well-known principle that if you can't see through a thing, it must be very deep. The makers of dirty windows therefore pay no heed to the inconvenient fact that even a mud puddle may be opaque.

And so it is scarcely strange that they have found a number of outlets for their talents. One is by the injection of foreign phrases, as when Ezra Pound heads one of his pieces with some words in French, and offers line nine in Greek; or when T. S. Eliot injects French, German and Italian into *The Waste Land*, and ends with this bit of wisdom:

Datta. Dayadhcam. Damyata.
Shantih   shantih   shantih

Writing of this sort, of course, serves two purposes. It proves the author to be erudite; and it enables him to write poetry merely by turning the pages of books in foreign languages. By simple copying, he can be tolerably sure of avoiding grammatical or other errors; but even if he does go astray, probably no one will discover the slip.

Not all writers of the dirty-window school, however, seem
to own books in foreign languages. Some prefer to do violence
to the English language; certain of their outpourings have
only the most distant relationship to words, as in the beginning of this from E. E. Cummings' *seventy-one poems*:

> after screamgroa
> ning:ish:ly;
> come
>
>   (s
>
> gruntsqueak
> , while
> idling-is-grindstone
> one; what: of, thumb

By no standard ever recognized in all the pre-Cummings
centuries can this be identified as poetry, or as prose, or as
anything but gibberish. But the publication of such work under
the imprint of one of the oldest and most respected university
presses, and its endorsement by many who sit in critical authority, show in what direction the apostles of dirty windows
are moving, and how strongly entrenched they are.

Here is another example, from a current verse magazine. I
quote only the beginning of William Newberry's *Postwar
Problem*, though there is more in the same vein:

> Dervish presses
> irradiate not

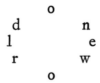

I confess that I am not sufficiently adept at cross-word puz-
zles to interpret these symbols. But the fact I should like to

bring out is that such mysterious jumbles are being seriously offered as *poetry* by journals that claim to represent the art of Shakespeare, Milton and Keats.

In all justice, however, we must admit that even the extremists rarely go this far. More often than not, they leave their windows only semi-darkened, as in Theodore Roethke's *Sensibility! O La!,* which opens thus:

> I'm the serpent of somebody else.
> See! She's sleeping like a lake:
> Glory to seize, I say.
>
> In the fair night of some dim brain,
> Thou wert marmorean-born.
> I name thee: wench of things,
> A true zephyr-haunted woodie.

This at least keeps company with words—except perhaps for "woodie," which my unabridged dictionary gives only as a humorous Scottish designation for "gallows."

Let us now turn to an example of a different type, and consider what might have happened if a poet of the old school had been a convert to the creed of dirty windows.

§ 2

Quite a bit more than a century ago, a great Englishman wrote two lines that might have been composed by a ploughman in the fields or a housewife in the kitchen:

> My heart leaps up when I behold
> A rainbow in the sky.

Were Wordsworth living today, and a disciple of the dirty-window school, he might disdain these clear and simple words in favor of something more in the mood of our times. Here is one possibility:

> A cardiac titillation
> tingling in my viscera
> agitates me
> at the sight of the sun-chemistry
> of solar colorations
> fragmented
> by the spectroscope of the clouds.

This, of course, though it does put considerable dirt on the window, is not altogether obscure. If the writer were to join a still more advanced group, he might turn out something like this:

> Me
> rainbow
> sky
> periscope
> tra, la, la.

Here, we might be told, is a work of subtle suggestion. Only one or two words are spoken—the reader is expected to surmise the rest. But what about the "periscope"? That, of course, is the subtlest device of all. It serves the useful purpose of putting a little more mist on the window.

Proceeding a trifle further, the author might give us something in this manner:

> r
> nbows
> gv me
> per
> pendic   ul ar   ly
> ver
> tcly

or
rec t ng ly
a pn
in th nck

Now the dust on the window is still deeper, although even yet it has not produced complete opacity.

But what about the original lines of the Lake Poet? — that lucid, beautiful and universal utterance, "My heart leaps up when I behold / A rainbow in the sky"! Obviously, while the windows were being smudged, the poetry was lost. And this, as in the crude but unfortunately not exaggerated examples given above, is the invariable result when dirty windows are deliberately sought.

But is it not true, a dissenter may ask, that great poems are not always as crystal-clear as Wordsworth's passage about the rainbow? Are they not sometimes complicated and difficult to interpret, and on occasions impossible to construe with exactness? What about the work of Chaucer, Spenser, Shakespeare, Donne, Blake, Browning, Poe and Swinburne, among others? Are these poets not now and then more than a little hard to follow ?

Paradoxically, in answering questions about dirty windows, it is necessary to see through clear windows. And if we attempt such clarity, what do we find? That there are four possible reasons, and only four, for obscurity in poetry or in any literary work:

(1). Changes produced by time in modes of expression or in the meaning of words.

(2). The inherent complexities of the subject-matter, defying the pen to surmount them.

(3). The incompetence, ineptitude or slovenliness of the author.

(4). The deliberate beclouding of meanings by the author, or the avoidance of meanings.

The first of the four causes—the changes in modes of expression or in the meaning of words—will account for most of the so-called dirty windows in Chaucer, Spenser and Shakespeare (though the latter, despite all the shifts in language, remains for the most part admirably lucid). The second source of obscurity—that which is due to the complexities of the subject-matter—is to be found in pieces such as Poe's *Ulalume* and Francis Thompson's *The Hound of Heaven,* as well as in many other mystical offerings. Here the obscurity, which is nearer to vagueness than to complete impenetrability, is inherent in the theme and cannot be dissociated from it by any effort of the author, who accepts it only because he cannot avoid it, and realizes that the merits of his work must be in spite of rather than because of the haziness that surrounds it. Consider the following:

> The gentle Light that shines behind the storm,
> The Dream that many a twilight hour enfolds.

These words by Eva Gore-Booth, which are typical of the sort of work mentioned above, may not be clear with a noonday distinctness; but how much more they convey than contemporary obscurity such as Edith Sitwell's "lynx-furred and lynx-purring plain of snow where branches of red coral / Hum of the spring to come," or than Dylan Thomas' "avalanche / Of the golden ghost who ringed with his streams her mercury bone"!

The third of the four sources of dirty windows—the incompetence, ineptitude or slovenliness of the author—may unfor-

tunately be found even among generally meritorious and sometimes otherwise great writers. Who will say that Donne,
though far more lucid than his modern imitators, was always
as clear as he would have been if gifted with greater talent,
willingness or skill? Who will assert that his rank below the
major poets is not due largely to his very failures in communication? Who will contend that Blake and Browning and the
others—all of whom could be compellingly clear at their best—
would not be better poets were they compellingly clear always?
Who will argue that if the mistiness of Swinburne's mellifluous
but interminable stanzas had given place to the clear-cut utterance of a few verses, he would not be a poet of wider appeal?
And why, in the case of any of these writers, should we of
today imitate faults rather than virtues, failures rather than
successes?

We now return to the last of the reasons for obscurity: the
author's deliberate beclouding or avoidance of meanings. There
may have been poets in past ages who indulged in intentional
window-blurring; but if so, they have been lost amid the very
obscurity they created. For, just as he who puts out his eyes
destroys his functions as a seeing man, so he who dims his windows courts the negation of his very purpose-in-being as an
author. Throughout the entire main stream of literature, we
can trace a struggle against obscurity—a struggle to break
down the formidable, the immense and sometimes insuperable
barriers that nature has imposed between mind and mind. Any
attempt at obscurity, therefore, represents a reversal of a time-
less trend, an assault on the very strongholds of literary cre-
ativeness, a rejection of the aims, intention, meaning and accomplishment of the entire lettered art as it has descended to us
from the time of Homer and before. Was any good ever accomplished by the intentional dirtying of windows? In order
to answer this query, let me ask another question. Was any

good ever accomplished by indigestion? Just as indigestion represents a malfunctioning of the bodily mechanism, so obscurity represents a malfunctioning of the literary mechanism. And the one derangement is precisely as much to be desired as the other.

Let the writer therefore keep this in mind: the object of all serious writing, whether in prose or verse, is communication—communication of thoughts, feelings, moods, imaginings or impressions. Such communication may be enhanced by suggestiveness, embellished by rhetoric, vivified by figures of speech or other literary ornamentation; but from the moment when the writer loses sight of the main purpose, from the moment when he subordinates communication to externals such as self-titillation or the striking of a pose, he has started on the sharp descent toward failure. And that is why it is necessary for poets to toil, toil, toil everlastingly to keep their windows clean. For dirty windows are among the measures of literary inadequacy. And clean windows are among the tests, though far from the only ones, of literary accomplishment.

VI

"How Original Need I Be?"

"Be original, Poet, be original!" is in effect a commandment that the aspiring verse-writer will hear nowadays wherever he turns. "Be original in your choice of words, your subject-matter, your technique! Be original from your opening line until the end!"

Now this may sound like good advice. But actually it is a thing strange to hear. To begin with, it is superfluous, since no one was ever original just because he was told to be, just as no one was ever wise or logical, kind or sensitive or musical-minded thanks to the orders of authority. We fulfill that which it is in us to fulfill; and we can do no more regardless of the counsel dinned into our ears. If we are not original, we are not, and so the matter ends; a color-blind man could distinguish between red and green as easily as we could take a step that set us off from our neighbors.

But if on the other hand we *are* original, we gain nothing from instructions to be what we are: originality is something much easier to discover from outside than from within; the original man is unlikely to think of himself as original, because he is as he is, and though the heavens fall he must act as he acts, and all that he does seems natural to him. Does he look upon a sand-storm, and see in it the whirling of the galaxies of heaven? Does he gaze at the columns of ants struggling up a wall, and observe the generations of man fighting their way up the barricades of civilization? Has he a mind that can delve into the caverns of the past and the hinterlands of the future, and range among the stars and nebulae as agilely as the thought of others can enter the next room? In all these cases he may be given credit for originality, but actually his imagination is so much a part of him that it comes without an effort. Again, is he in the habit of seeing strange, little observed comparisons in common things, so that old stumps will take the shape of bears, and bees' eyes become sphinx eyes, and lumbering beetles are colored carts trundling along a road? If so, he is indeed original, but he will be the last to realize the fact, for it will not come to him that not everyone sees as he does. And his originality, if it finds expression in poetry, may be his most conspicuous quality, but he will not know that, since it will be something he did not strive to attain.

But what would happen to this man if, despite his inborn originality, he were to listen to the modern mandates, and not understanding what gifts he actually had, tried to reach for gifts he had not, and sought to be original in ways that nature had not meant? Instead of giving full scope to his natural perceptions, to the imagination and the unique vision that came to him as his birthright, he would try to follow the lead of the critics by being different along new lines. He might, for example, distort the shape of his poems, breaking up the verses to resemble diamonds or water jugs; he might introduce strange, unnatural or paradoxical expressions: "dark light," "bright darkness," "purple lightning," "black snow," "white coal," "heavy feathers," "feathery mercury" and other things that never were on heaven or earth outside the rhymes of current self-styled originals. But would this really be originality?

The sad fact is that many persons nowadays seem unable to distinguish between originality and eccentricity, between honest self-expression and showmanship. They seem to imagine that all an artist need do, in order to prove originality, is to throw off his outer garments in a crowded street, and begin dancing the hula. In other words, in order to be original he must make a display of himself; he must attract attention. The hula dancer on a crowded street certainly *is* different—

that is to say, different from ordinary sane and sober people. But he is different in the way of the ancient Greek who, according to legend, despaired of attaining fame by normal means, and so made himself infamous by setting fire to a temple. Exhibitionists have always been with us, and no doubt always will be so long as talentless men are obsessed with an ambition to shine; but there is no reason why they should be regarded more seriously than the small boy showing off before his elders. Nevertheless, many current exhibitionists *have been* taken seriously.

The quotations made in the last chapter, from writers who introduce foreign phrases and give us distorted and wordless jumbles in the name of poetry, are examples of the modern disease miscalled originality. And other instances are not hard to find. We observe them in the English writer Terence Heywood, who in his book *How Smoke Got Into the Air,* offers page after page filled with lines like these:

> "BLINDMOUTH" of Milton, Samsonseeingstone,
> Shakespearesynopting-lovechains-easily-smasht,
> Beethovenhearingthroughanemptyear
> crystals-as-perfect, shuttered in a TEAR,
> ARC-Of-ALL-Sound, the Arc of Preservation . . .
> Troyinallashes, Londonsinacrash . . .

If this is originality, it is the kind to be found behind the bars of any asylum.

Not going nearly so far, but likewise striking a pose in the effort to prove originality, are the offerings of one who has been acclaimed a leading American poet. I quote the opening of one of Marianne Moore's typical pieces, *Four Quartz Crystal Clocks,* in the version given in her *Collected Poems:*

> There are four vibrators, the world's exactest clocks;
>   and these quartz time-pieces that tell

time intervals to other clocks,
    these worksless clocks work well;
independently the same, kept in
    the 41° Bell
        Laboratory time

vault. Checked by a comparator with Arlington,
    they punctualize the 'radio,
cinema,' and 'presse,'—a group the
    Giraudoux truth-bureau
of hoped-for accuracy has termed
'instruments of truth.' . . .

In order to understand just what the author has done, let us transpose this as follows:

There are four vibrators, the world's exactest clocks; and these quartz time-pieces that tell time intervals to other clocks, these worksless clocks work well; independently the same, kept in the 41° Bell laboratory time vault. Checked by a comparator with Arlington, they punctualize the 'radio, cinema,' and 'presse'—a group the Giraudoux truth-bureau of hoped-for accuracy has termed 'instruments of truth.'

Viewed in this form, the miserable sham stands exposed. We see that the writer, without the flimsiest claim to originality (and without the flimsiest claim to poetry), has struck an attitude in order to prove herself original and poetic. The attitude she has struck, of course, is the puerile one of offering the work separated into lines with a visual resemblance to poetry. Actually, there is not the shadow of a reason for these lines as she has divided them, and least of all for the shabby trick of splitting "time vault" between two stanzas. Her work, printed as prose, shows itself to be nothing but prose, and undistinguished prose at that. And her originality proves to be counterfeit.

This, therefore, will indicate one of the pitfalls against which the writer should be on guard. Originality, after all, is more than a matter of typography.

§ 2

Like many other good things, originality is not always what you would expect it to be. It does not shout to make itself known; it does not glare or blare; it neither gesticulates nor wears a mask, but goes quietly on its way, content to be seen or not seen. Its hallmark is not the fantastic posture, the bizarre turn of phrase, the shocking subject-matter; it rarely visits the writer who heaves and puffs for effect, but may come to him who utters himself as simply and unlaboriously as the dandelion shining from the grass. It is not a mark of originality to write with a pretentious turgidness and a deliberate juxtaposition of incongruous elements, as Dylan Thomas has done in these lines:

> What is the meter of the dictionary?
> The size of genesis? the short spark's gender?
> Shade without shape? the shape of Pharaoh's echo?
> (My shape of age nagging the wounded whisper).
> Which sixth of wind blew out the burning gentry?
> (Questions are hunchbacks to the poker marrow).

This is trick writing, and almost (though Thomas' followers will deny this) formula writing, since it follows a plain prescription: to associate things that cannot naturally be associated. It requires no great ingenuity, and no originality at all, to carry on indefinitely in this vein. For example, with no claims whatever to poetic accomplishment, I offer the following:

> What is the starlight of Limburger cheese?
> The temperature of rhythms? the deep cold's sex-life?
> Tone without sound? the sound of Caesar's shadow?
> (My sound of verse begging the tortured color).

Which ninth of flame burned out the blowing Thomases?
(Poems are halfbacks to the poker cerebrum).

If this sounds like nonsense, the reason is clear; it *is* nonsense. But it is not one iota the more original for having taken leave of its wits. To the undiscriminating, however, it may *seem* original because hard if not impossible to fathom. And exactly the same may be said of the passage by Thomas. With manifest effort and frantic contortions of expression, he has strained to prove himself original. And he has only proved his lack of that true originality which comes without strain.

For an example of genuine originality, consider Burns' *To A Mouse, On Turning Her Up In Her Nest With the Plough,* with its well-known opening stanza:

> Wee, skeetit, cow'rin, tim'rous beastie,
> Oh, what a panic's in thy breastie!
> Thou need na start awa sae hasty,
>   Wi' bickering brattle!
> I wad be laith to run an' chase thee,
>   Wi' murd'ring pattle!

To have such a feeling for a small helpless creature of the field, and to express the feeling in simple and artless-seeming verse—that is originality, for it represents the truthful expression of the man's deeper self, a self not quite like that of his neighbors, nor indeed like that of any other being on earth. Because he had something of his own to say, because he both thought and felt, he had an original poem to offer—and that without threshing about him for far-fetched modes of expression, striking and truthless paradoxes, and rare and tormented combinations of words and ideas.

Coleridge, likewise, was original, richly and unforgettably so, when he embodied his love for the world's creatures in one of the great ballads of all time, a ballad whose expression, though often striking, keeps to the simplicity of the lines that epitomize its thought:

> He prayeth best, who loveth best
> All things both great and small;
> For the dear God who loveth us,
> He made and loveth all.

Note that there is here not one remarkable word or phrase, even though the whole is highly original.

Turning to that most commonplace of themes, human love, Browning likewise uses not a word or phrase except of the most usual, and yet produces a line of striking originality:

> O lyric love, half angel and half bird.

And Wordsworth, writing of the things of nature that moved him so deeply, has given us in *Tintern Abbey* one of the most magnificent and original passages of blank verse in the language:

> . . . a sense sublime
>
> Of something far more deeply interfused,
> Whose dwelling is the light of setting suns,
> And the round ocean, and the living air,
> And the blue sky, and in the mind of man;
> A motion and a spirit, that impels
> All thinking things, all objects of all thought,
> And rolls through all things.

Wordsworth did not here have to look for originality; he already had it. And he already had it because he had lived it, thought it, felt it, and hence had no need to swing his hands in wild circles and lift his voice in knotted opacities in order to prove it his. Observe that he is content with the simplest phrases: "round ocean," "living air," "blue sky," "mind of man." But the whole is no less original and no less impressive because he did not seek a more novel "square ocean," "dead air," "spinach sky," or "cranium of *homo sapiens*."

Much the same, as our discussion will have indicated, is true of originality in subject-matter. The original writer is not he who, merely because no other poet has ever attacked the theme, descants upon street sweepers or ash cans, the star Ursae Majoris, the protozoans known as *Choanoflagellata,* or the sponge *Hippospongia lapidescens turrita.* The original writer is the one who discusses in verse anything whatever which is so close to him that the expression simply bursts out. I am not asserting that an original writer may not discourse upon street sweepers, the star Ursae Majoris or the sponge *Hippospongia;* all that I am saying is that no one can be original as a result of selecting these themes in order to be original. On the contrary, he can be original only if the theme, in a sense, selects him. Blake, visualizing the dread prowler of the jungle so clearly that it actually becomes part of his consciousness, can produce something so strangely original as

> Tiger! Tiger! burning bright
> In the forests of the night!

But a modern writer, not visualizing the great striped beast and trying to be original, would be more likely to end with something like

> The leaping interrogation point
> with eyes like two-hundred watt searchlights
> burned through the blackout
> vacancies.

This, however, is not original, for it is not felt, and has no true relation to the tiger. This is merely a manufactured product, a strained effort to be original. And no one in the long run is likely to be valued as original unless he can distinguish between strained efforts and those impulses, based upon real feeling and profound experience, which gush from the depths like irrepressible fountains.

VII

The Heart And The Head

Throughout all the centuries, the heart has played a greater part in human affairs than the head. Man's passions, much more than his reasoning mind, have stimulated the motions and convulsions of peoples, have incited wars and kindled revolutions, have set the spark to factional strife, pillage and assassination, and have inspired migrations and driven men to wild adventures and hopeless quests for freedom. The head, when called upon at all, has at best played a cautious and often a little regarded second. And this is no less true in individual affairs, in which the head has been subordinate and usually helpless before the frenzies of love and hatred, pain and grief, pride and ambition, desire, prejudice, envy, rage and revenge.

And if these forces have dominated human life, inevitably they have governed literature. From the earliest utterances of the race, the emotional element has prevailed: we see this abundantly, for example, in the *Iliad*, in the very theme of the abduction and attempted recovery of Helen of Troy, in the sulking of Achilles, in his exultation at Hector's death and in the vainglory with which he drags the body of his fallen enemy behind his chariot wheels. We see it, too, in the frequent appeals to men's pride, as when Ajax calls upon the Argives either to die or to beat off doom from their galleys. And we see it in the many outbreaks of grief, as when the mother of Achilles bursts into wailing at the sorrow that has fallen upon her son, or when the parents of Hector moan and bewail their child's tragic fate. The *Iliad*, throughout its length, is an emotional poem. And were it not so, it would have had far less appeal for its own day and for a later age.

The same may be said of all great literature. The woes of Queen Dido in the *Aeneid* are proverbial, as are the tears of

Tasso and the lamentations of Job; and the feelings of the heart, its sorrow and its exaltation, are likewise evident in the work of the old English and Scottish balladists, as we see in emotional expressions such as

> And, oh! that my young babe was born
> And set upon my nurse's knee,
> And I myself were dead and gane!
> And the green grass growing over me,

and this from another ballad:

> I wish I were where Helen lies!
> Night and day on me she cries,
> And I am weary of the skies,
>   For her sake that died for me.

Not that all emotion flows in this morbid vein, but that emotion and expression may be connected intimately even when no cerebral element is visible at all. In poetry especially, and in lyrical poetry most obviously, emotion has been of the essence of creation. It is impossible to imagine Burns without the feelings that give sweetness and poignancy to his songs; and it is equally impossible to imagine most of Shakespeare's sonnets stripped of emotion. Take, for example, the one beginning,

> When, in disgrace with fortune and men's eyes,
> I all alone beweep my outcast state,
> And trouble deaf heaven with my bootless cries,
> And look upon myself, and curse my fate . . .

Similarly, many of the Elizabethan songs would be impossible without emotion, as Ben Jonson's *On My First Son*, "Farewell, thou child of my right hand, and joy!", and Tichborne's *Elegy*, written in the Tower before his execution in

1586, and Daniel's moving sonnet beginning "Care-charmer Sleep, son of the sable night," with lines such as

> And let the day be time enough to mourn
> The shipwreck of my ill-adventured youth:
> Let waking eyes suffice to wail their scorn,
> Without the torment of the night's untruth.

In later poetry, the story is much the same. Even a writer who (at his worst) can be so matter-of-fact and cerebral as Wordsworth, illustrates at his best the truth of his own statement that poetry is "emotion recollected in tranquility":

> She lived alone, and few could know
>   When Lucy ceased to be;
> But she is in her grave, and oh,
>   The difference to me!

Or take this from one of Wordsworth's sonnets:

> Why art thou silent! Is thy love a plant
> Of such weak fibre that the treacherous air
> Of absence withers what was once so fair?

Since sorrow is one of the most powerful emotions, it is particularly in evidence in poetry. But other emotions, as every poetry lover knows, are also common. Sometimes a poem may glow with a gently exalted sentiment, as in Wordsworth's sonnet *Upon Westminster Bridge,* in which we feel the very pulse of tranquility:

> Never did sun more beautifully steep
>   In his first splendour valley, rock, or hill;
> Ne'er saw I, never felt, a calm so deep!

Sometimes the emotion is sweetly nostalgic for the irrevocable past, as in Longfellow's *My Lost Youth*:

> Often I think of the beautiful town
>   That is seated by the sea,

Often in thought go up and down
The pleasant streets of that dear old town,
And my youth comes back to me.

Sometimes the nostalgia is for something still existing, as
in Browning's *Home-Thoughts from Abroad,* and sometimes
the mood is that of a fierce exultation. Take James Elroy
Flecker's *War Song of the Saracens*:

We are they who ride faster than fate: we are they
    who ride early or late:
We storm at your ivory gate: pale Kings of the Sunset,
    beware!

Sometimes the poet's passion bespeaks an inner war and
conquest, but is no less powerful for that reason, as Emily
Bronte has proved:

Then dawns the Invisible; the Unseen its truth reveals;
My outward sense is gone, my inward essence feels:
Its wings are almost free—its home, its harbour found,
Measuring the gulf, it stoops and dares the final bound.

Oh! dreadful is the check—intense the agony—
When the ear begins to hear, and the eye begins to see;
When the pulse begins to throb, the brain to think again;
The soul to feel the flesh, and the flesh to feel the chain.

Sometimes, again, the emotion is of infinite longing, infinite
desire, as in Tennyson's well-known lines:

O that 'twere possible
After long grief and pain
To find the arms of my true love
Round me once again!

Even so reflective a poem as the *Rubaiyat* of Omar Khayyam is packed with emotion:

> I sometimes think that never blows so red
> The Rose as where some buried Caesar bled;
>   That every Hyacinth the Garden wears
> Dropt on her Lap from some once lovely Head.

And emotion pulses through the pages of one of the most beautifully meditative of all English poems, *In Memoriam*:

> Dark house, by which once more I stand
>   Here in the long unlovely street,
>   Doors, where my heart was used to beat
> So quickly, waiting for a hand,
>
> A hand that can be clasped no more . . .

And in our own day emotion in poetry is far from dead. Walter de la Mare, one of the best of modern lyric writers, has shown it frequently, as in this from the poem to his mother:

> Never in twilight comes the moon to me,
> Stealing thro' these far woods, but tells of thee,
>   Falls, dear, on my wild heart,
>   And takes thy part.

Even more subtly, we find emotion in de la Mare's ghost poem *Winter Dusk*, in which a mother reads to her children, unaware of the *revenant*, not realizing that, as she read to two, " 'Twas surely three who heard":

> Yet when, the story done, she smiled,
> From face to face, serene and clear,
> A love, half dread, sprang up, as she
>   Leaned close and drew them near.

And Masefield, another of our century's outstanding poets, has saturated his work with emotion. We find this in his early songs, with the simple longing of pieces like *Sea Fever*, "I must go down to the seas again, to the lonely sea and the sky." And we discover it in his long narratives and contemplative sonnets:

> When this my life will be a dream outdreamt;
> And one, remembering friendship by the fire,
> And one, remembering love time in the dark,
> And one, remembering unfulfilled desire,
> Will sigh . . .

But there is no need to go on indefinitely. From the above examples, it will be evident how emotion has interfused itself into the structure of poetry and especially of lyrical poetry throughout the generations (the most notable exception being in the age of Pope and Dryden, an age which, like our own, was drily rational, and in which, as in our own, poetry declined).

In the face of all this, it is curious to find emotion now under a cloud; to hear the apostles of "modernism" warning us against it, directing us to make our work "objective" and "cerebral" in defiance of the practice and the experience of millennia. But it is more curious still to see the new commandments actually being followed—followed to such an extent that emotion in the work of many of the new writers is as hard to find as roses in a salt-marsh.

Truly, to one who glances back at three thousand years of literature, this is most confusing; and to the young writer it must be bewildering. What therefore, one must ask, are the incentives behind the new movement? What have been its results? What sort of a model does it offer for the youthful aspirant?

§ 2

There is a sense in which the revolt against emotion represents a rebellion against everything old, everything antedating our own generation. And there is a sense in which it is but another indication of the "modernist's" almost morbid sensitiveness to the hackneyed and the trite. But beyond all this, the latter-day attitude is to some degree a reaction to genuine abuses, to that disease of sentiment known as "sentimentality," and to pseudo-emotional outpourings of the nature of onion tears. Let us admit that some poets—and also some prose writers—have been ready to pour out the tears by the basinful. We have all encountered would-be pathetic utterances which are really bathetic, "Oh! Oh! Oh! Oh, my heart! Oh, my heart!"—manifestly, a case in which "The lady doth protest too much," since people suffering genuine sorrow do not exclaim in this fashion, but will more likely show their grief (if they do not conceal it entirely) by a word, a sigh, a silence, an unconscious gesture.

But because inept or insincere writers rant and rave, with explosions of mock emotion, are we to conclude that there is no true emotion? — that all emotion must be ruled out of poetry? It would be as logical to decide that, because there have been corrupt magistrates, we should abolish the law courts. The obvious remedy, of course, is to weed out the make-believe emotion, and not to close the doors on the genuine. Yet this obvious course has not been taken.

The resentment against pseudo-emotion, however, does not nearly explain the outlawry of all emotion. The dominating cause, I believe, goes deeper, and has its roots in the general philosophy of the literary sophisticates, and, to a lesser degree, in the philosophy of the age. The real foundation is a materialistic interpretation of life, a mechanistic explanation of the universe and of man, and a consequent disbelief in the existence of the individual soul and the worth of individuality. For if the individual soul be only a fiction of the sentimentalists, and if man be a mere bit of clever mechanism that is wound up and soon runs out forever, then it is preposterous to permit any play of personal emotion, for what is there worth being emotional about? Emotion, if by chance it does crop up, is a mere physical upwelling, not to be taken seriously; it had best be treated ironically, as a father treats the babbling of babes.

It is some such attitude which, judging by all the evidence, the modern literati have embraced. That their philosophy is as shallow as their poetry, their pretended insights justified neither by science nor by logic, are points that might be argued indefinitely; but they are points that are largely irrelevant, since the critic has no right to impose his cosmic or general beliefs upon the writer, whether these are valid or not. There would be just as much excuse, let us say, for authorities who disliked England or France to rule that nothing French or English should ever be mentioned in poetry; or for authorities who disbelieved in religion to proclaim the day of religious verse forever past. He who has prejudices or preconceptions may include them in his own work; but if he ordains them for the work of others, his commands will verge upon tyranny.

Now let us see how the principles of the icicle school have fared in practice. Every reader of up-to-date magazines and books of verse knows the results, for he has opportunity to observe little else. The typical work stirs the feelings in about the way that one's sense of delight is roused by these lines on *Joy*, from a well-known monthly of verse:

> Transfixed on paper the butterfly thought
> Blinks on a pin. All is well.

Or else they resemble these, from *Invocation,* in the same magazine:

> Monstrous, enigma, paradox, the rope
> with a horn on its hang, holding the center,
> burning the air with its bellows, as the air
> bells back, the taunt becoming a spire.

This may be "cerebral" verse, but the cerebration is of a sort that most of us cannot be expected to follow.

Let us take another example: the beginning of *Tract,* by William Carlos Williams:

> I will teach you my townspeople
> how to perform a funeral—
> for you have it over a troupe
> of artists—
> unless one should scour the world—
> you have the ground sense necessary.

By his scoffing, casual attitude toward a ceremony that can evoke the profoundest emotions and that all ages and peoples have treated with reverence, the author here does his best to show his contempt for the hearts of men. Incidentally, since he is not only a verse-maker but a physician, who must often have encountered the awesome spectacle of death, his attitude strikes one as particularly unfeeling.

One finds suggestions of the same state of mind in the work of another versifying physician, Merrill Moore, who includes the following in his *Verse Diary of a Psychiatrist:*

> More than once I have made this mistake:
> I did not realize that my patient was dying
> So I spent too much energy in trying
> To hold off death. . . .

> Now I realize that I truly ought
> To have not done this so I have changed my ways
> And when I know (that is, *know positively*)
> There is no hope and that the Reaper comes
> Without the menace of advancing drums
> I stand by quietly and let him come;
> The answer is an equilibrium.

You might suppose that the author was recording a chemical reaction, or at most the passing of a beetle, instead of the culminating drama in the life of a thinking, pulsating, suffering human being—a drama that may leave unknown echoes and repercussions upon other lives, and even affect the future of a community or a nation. It may indeed be true that "The answer is an equilibrium," but certainly not an equilibrium between poetry and the normal sentiments of normal mankind.

This attitude of unhuman and almost anti-human coldness, to be sure, is not confined to our medical verse-writers. A similar outlook is exhibited by many, including Wallace Stevens, who in *The Mechanical Optimist* makes a sort of nursery rhyme out of diabetes:

> A lady dying of diabetes
> Listened to the radio,
> Catching the lesser dithyrambs.
> So heaven collects its bleating lambs.
>
> Accompanied by the exegesis
> Of familiar things in a cheerful voice,
> Like the night before Christmas and all its carols.
> Dying lady, rejoice, rejoice!

From this you might gather that dying of diabetes is a little like going to a party.

It would not, of course, be just to imply that writers of the new school are predominantly concerned with such an ancient and fundamental (and therefore trite) fact as dying. More often they are content to elaborate general philosophies, whose temperature need not be much above absolute zero. Oscar Williams gives us an example in *The New Sphinx,* opening thus:

> The new sphinx with lips of economics
> Propounds the question, the gears grinding in the throat:
> —What is reality?—and the man with the demon skin
> Lets his amorphous eyes upward toward Paradise float.
>
> And with wet seas of astonishment he now beholds
> The insect glitterings of the amorphous sphere,
> Huge foreign body trafficking in the blood stream,
> Shrieking and disgorging the synthetic year.

It is safe to say that this will never make one pulse beat the faster. And we may question whether it will add much more to the world's wisdom than to its sentiment.

Here is still another example, which likewise illustrates the tendency of writers of the heart-less school to be as impersonal in mentioning human beings as in depicting worms or wood. The selection is by E. E. Cummings, and is a piece that anthologists apparently value especially, since they reprint it so frequently. I quote the beginning of *My Sweet Old Etcetera:*

> My sweet old etcetera
> aunt lucy during the recent
>
> war could and what
> is more did tell you just
> what everybody was fighting
>
> for,
> my sister
>
> isabel created hundreds
> (and
> hundreds) of socks not to

mention shirts fleaproof earwarmers
etcetera wristers etcetera . . .

If you have a tingling suspicion that this is not poetry, you may well reflect upon Ezra Pound's reference to "the dead art / Of Poetry," and Marianne Moore's candid remark, "I too dislike it: there are things that are important beyond all this fiddle." Certainly, there are things that are important beyond all the "fiddle" quoted above; one has the feeling that the very authors despise their own work—and if so, who can blame them? But if the authors despise their own work, how can the readers be expected to respect it?

T. S. Eliot, though he doubtless had not this especial situation in mind, has summarized it aptly in one of his own characteristically frigid offerings:

> We are the hollow men
> We are the stuffed men
> Leaning together
> Headpiece filled with straw. Alas!
> Our dried voices, when
> We whisper together
> Are quiet and meaningless
> As wind in dry grass
> Or rats' feet over broken glass
> In our dry cellar . . .

My mind runs back over the course of a generation, and, strangely, the names come to me of many who once wrote verse of a cold variety—though not always quite of the present iceberg temperature—before most of today's cold lights had blinked into prominence. Who, I wonder, now reads *Some Imagist Poets*, by "H. D." and John Gould Fletcher? Who settles down for a pleasant evening with "H. D.'s" *Sea Garden*, or Fletcher's *Preludes and Symphonies*, or Alfred Kreymborg's *Mushrooms*, or the verses of Jeanne D'Orge, Walter Conrad

Arenberg, Wallace Gould, Mina Loy, Maxwell Bodenheim, or even the once-celebrated Amy Lowell? These and many like them have come, and have passed or are passing; and the central reason for their lack of appeal, I believe, is their failure to strike a responsive chord in the reader's heart.

And, similarly, any new poet who fails to warm the heart may sputter for a moment with the eccentric brilliance of a rocket bursting, but the sparks will swiftly flare out, the ashes will drift to earth, and in the eyes of tomorrow he will not exist.

VIII

The Ever-Burning Lamp

A few scores of thousands of years ago, on some undated day in some land now nameless, a youth stood on a promontory of the ocean or the brow of a hill, and stared out over the wide colored landscapes of the world. And a sense of awe overcame him, and a wonder, and a delight mixed with reverence for something beyond him that seemed greater than he and yet somehow entered his being and became part of him. And thus for the first time, though he had not yet given it a name, man worshipped at the altar-stairs of beauty.

Perhaps in the same general period of the world's history, another youth stared in marveling joy at a field of wildflowers, at a sunset cloud, at a waterfall, or into the eyes of his beloved, and flung out his arms with a sense of the glory of life. And again man had kept a rendezvous with the goddess beauty. And still another savage was enchanted with the sound of the tribal chant, and made ecstatic new rhythms; and still another called forth sweet tones by blowing through a river reed—and once more beauty had called to man.

What that beauty was, man did not know. And though ages have passed, and the hairy primitive has given place to the gloved sophisticate, we still do not know. But this we do know: that as man advanced and art and literature developed, the intangible known as beauty moved him more and more. In time it swayed the brush of the painter and the chisel of the sculptor; it guided the architect, the dancer and the musician; it became the unseen guardian of poetry and prose.

Nevertheless, what *is* beauty? Though the disquisitions on aesthetics have been many, we cannot answer with the defininiteness with which we measure wood or stone. We can suggest that beauty is something in the spiritual essence of the universe speaking to the spirit of man; that it is the language of the deeper truth of things. But we can be most specific by pointing to the manifestations of beauty. It is the first red signal flare of dawn, and the last crimson ember of dusk. It is the tender yellow-green of bursting maple leaves, and the gold and scarlet of those same leaves on the winds of autumn. It is the magnificence of stars and mountains, and the glossy deep-orange of a single wild poppy. It is the graceful curve of lips and brows, and the thunder surge of the organ; it is the solid structure of temple columns, and the structureless lilt of a song; it is the stuff of shadows and fantasies and dreams, yet is the ever-burning lamp that sparkles across the centuries. At the peak of human attainment—in the Athens of Pericles, the Florence of the Renaissance, the England of the first Elizabeth—beauty has been enthroned though its very name may have been unspoken, and its enthronement was associated with man's rarest achievements.

Already in the dawning centuries of literature, we find poetry fired with beauty. We see this in Egypt and Palestine; we see it in Greece, from Homer and the idylls of Theocritus through the works of the dramatists and the later lyric writers. Beauty beckons to us even in translation from this fragment of Sappho, in the version of Lord Byron:

> O Hesperus, thou bringest all good things—
> Home to the weary, to the hungry cheer,
> To the young bird the parent's brooding wings,
> The welcome stall to the o'erlabored steer;
> Whate'er of peace about our hearthstone clings,
> Whate'er our household gods protect of dear,
> Are gathered round us by thy look of rest;
> Thou bring'st the child too to its mother's breast.

And we can feel the very pulse of beauty in William Cory's often-quoted translation of Callimachus' lines on Heraclitus:

> They told me, Heraclitus, they told me you were dead,
> They brought me bitter news to hear and bitter tears to shed.
> I wept as I remembered how often you and I
> Had tired the sun with talking and sent him down the sky.
>
> And now that thou art lying, my dear old Carian guest,
> A handful of gray ashes, long, long ago at rest,
> Still are thy pleasant voices, thy nightingales, awake;
> For Death, he taketh all away, but them he cannot take.

Here the rhythm is in part the source of the beauty, which springs more largely, however, from the sentiment and its felicitous expression. Strange, is it not, that beauty can arise from grief and bereavement quite as readily as from wonder and exultation!

Throughout the ages, this indescribable glory has continued to dominate poetry, often as an unconscious undertone, occasionally rising almost to the status of a cult. Poets of the old school have not hesitated to acknowledge their indebtedness to beauty, as in the well-known lines of Keats, "A thing of beauty is a joy forever," and "Beauty is truth, truth beauty, that is all / Ye know on earth, and all ye need to know." And Andrew Lang, in *A Sonnet to Heavenly Beauty* (a translation from the sixteenth century Frenchman, Joachim Du Bellay), recognizes beauty as an emanation or a reflection from some diviner realm:

> . . . in the most highest heavens shalt thou
> Behold the very Beauty, whereof now
> Thou worshippest the shadow upon earth.

One of the best of recent poets, Arthur Davison Ficke, does not hesitate to speak of beauty repeatedly: for example, in these lines from *Sonnets of a Portrait Painter*:

> Your beauty is as timeless as the earth;
> All storied women live again in you,

and,

> I have seen beauty where light stabs the hills
> Gold-shafted through a cloud of rosy stain.

More strikingly yet, in a sonnet of *Tumultuous Shore*, Ficke
pays his respects to his goddess:

> Beauty can be the reawakening spell
> For wonders that the spirit always knew—
> Or the strange coming of a miracle . . .
> As the heart sees, with dim incredulous eyes,
> Itself the manger where a saviour lies.

And John Masefield, whose sonnets are saturated with beauty,
uses the name with an unhesitating frequency:

> Be with me, Beauty, for the fire is dying
>
>   *   *   *
>
> Whatever beauty has been quick in clay,
> Some effluence of it lives
>
>   *   *   *
>
> Beauty, let be; I cannot see your face,
> I shall not know you now, nor touch your feet
>
>   *   *   *
>
> If I could come again to that dear place
> Where once I came, where Beauty lived and moved
>
>   *   *   *
>
> Here in the self is all that man can know
> Of Beauty, all the wonder, all the power . . .

These are but a few references out of many; nor do they
represent lip-service only, for beauty haunts all Masefield's
lines in which she is mentioned:

> Or does sweet Beauty dwell in lovely things,
> Scattering the holy hintings of her name

In women, in dear friends, in flowers, in springs,
In the brook's voice, for us to catch the same?
Or is it we who are Beauty, we who ask,
We by whose gleams the world fulfills its task?

Likewise in the themes chosen by poets, we see homage paid to beauty, from the allegorical enchantments of *The Fairie Queene* to the equally fantastic charms of Arnold's *The Forsaken Merman*, and from the statuesque grandeur of *Paradise Lost* to the legendary *Wanderings of Oisin* and *Baile and Ailinn* of Yeats. The rhythms of poetry, too, from the stateliness of blank verse through the swinging lyricism of a Poe or Swinburne to the august stride of the great makers of odes and sonnets, have done reverence to beauty. And the lines and passages that shine by their beauty are innumerable. One thinks of utterances such as "Full many a glorious morning have I seen / Flatter the mountain-tops with sovereign eye," and "The holy time is quiet as a nun / Breathless with adoration," and "Verse, a breeze 'mid blossoms straying, / Where Hope clung feeding like a bee," and "Ye stars! which are the poetry of Heaven!", and ". . . the painted veil which those who live/Call life," and "He is a portion of that loveliness/Which once he made more lovely," and "Joy, whose hand is ever at his lips / Bidding adieu," and "I have seen old ships sail like swans asleep / Beyond the village which men still call Tyre," and, finally, "The ground-whirl of the perished leaves of Hope, / The wind of Death's imperishable wing."

The list might be prolonged indefinitely, but these are the sort of lines which poets before our own day have offered us in worship of beauty—loveliness linked to meaning. In contrast, what do the typical "modernists" put forth? I quote some examples, which, occurring in a recent anthology of modern verse, have had a measure of critical approval: " 'Why,' said a bored numerologist, reaching for his hat, 'can't these star-gazers keep their feet on the ground?'" (Kenneth Fearing). "Lots of truisms don't have to be repeated but there is one that has got to be." (Ogden Nash). "Kicking his mother until she let go of his soul / Has given him a healthy appetite." (W. H. Auden). "Consider his life which was valueless / In terms of employment, hotel ledgers, news files." (Stephen Spender). "I am haunted by interrupted acts / introspective as a leper, enchanted / by a repulsive clew." (Muriel Rukeyser). "Not only how far away, but the way you say it / Is very important." (Henry Reed). "We, the symmetrians, seek justice here / And asymettric nature seeks a drought" (Gene Derwood).

Again the list might be prolonged indefinitely. I must concede, of course, that these lines do not surpass their authors' average level; whereas the first quotations glow by a special light of their own. All very true! but you could search long in the work of the last-quoted authors without finding much more of beauty than in the lines given above. They do not write as if (to quote one of them) "The way you say it is very important." Nor do they write as if what they say is important, or as if beauty counts in the least. They write as if they had no sense or realization of beauty, though in some cases they do seem to have a well-developed sense of ugliness. And for that reason among others (one of the others being the usual lack of a recognizable poetic rhythm) their work falls to the valley level of prose, and is flat, unilluminated, and uninspiring.

But let us apply a different test. Let us see how similar themes have been handled, first, by the beauty-scorning modern, and, secondly, by the beauty-loving traditionalist. We may begin with the opening lines of John Crowe Ransom's *Here Lies a Lady*, which, though written with conventional meter and rhyme, treats death in the standard flippant and unemo-

tional and hence unbeautiful manner of the contemporary
school:

>Here lies a lady of beauty and high degree.
>Of chills and fever she died, of fever and chills,
>The delight of her husband, her aunts, and an infant of three,
>And of medicos marveling sweetly on her ills.

Now take Edna St. Vincent Millay's *Elegy Before Death,* in
which a similar theme occurs. I quote the opening and concluding lines:

>There will be rose and rhododendron
>　　When you are dead and under ground;
>Still will be heard from white syringias
>　　Heavy with bees, a sunny sound.

>　　　　　*　　*　　*

>Oh, there will pass with your great passing
>　　Little of beauty not your own,—
>Only the light from common water.
>Only the grace from simple stone.

Can there be any question that the second quotation has the
impact of poetry, and the first has not?

Now consider another pair of examples. The following is
from Lloyd Frankenberg's *The Sea*:

>Imposing its single structure on the sky
>and drawing thence its variable mood
>of bright confusion, gloom and equable
>conformity, the ocean goes scotfree
>of other obligation but to pay
>the moon its due respects, discharged like spouse.

By contrast, I am tempted to quote the entire fourth sonnet
from George Sterling's *Sonnets by the Night Sea,* beginning

"The wind of night is like an ocean's ghost." But for the sake of brevity, I confine myself to the sestet:

> Yea! and the Deep is troubled! In this heart
> Are voices of a far and shadowy Sea,
> Above whose wastes no lamp of earth shall gleam.
> Farewells are spoken and the ships depart
> For that horizon and its mystery
> Whose stars tell not if life, or death, is dream.

Here, with the hallmark of beauty and imagination, we have that yearning suggestiveness which can be one of the great values of poetry. But of this there is not a trace in Mr. Frankenberg.

Now turn from the sea to one of the creatures of the sea. Here is how Elizabeth Bishop opens her *The Fish*:

> I caught a tremendous fish
> and held him beside the boat
> half out of water, with my hook
> fast in a corner of his mouth.
> He didn't fight.
> He hadn't fought at all.
> He hung a grunting weight,
> battered and venerable
> and homely. . . .

And here is how a twentieth century traditionalist, Rupert Brooke, describes a fish:

> In a cool curving world he lies
> And ripples with dark ecstasies.
> The kind luxurious lapse and steal
> Shapes all the universe to feel
> And know and be; the clinging stream
> Closes his memory, glooms his dream,
> Who lips the roots o' the shore, and glides

> Superb on unreturning tides.
> Those silent waters weave for him
> A fluctuant mutable world and dim . . .

And now for a final pair of examples. Let us see how a "modern" and a traditionalist face the great basic theme of man and mortality. The first opens the title poem of Marianne Moore's collection, *What Are Years?*:

> What is our innocence,
> what is our guilt? All are
> naked, none is safe. And whence
> is courage: the unanswered question,
> the resolute doubt,—
> dumbly calling, deafly listening—that
> in misfortune, even death,
>   encourages others
>   and in its defeat, suits
>   the soul to be strong? He
> sees deep and is glad, who
>   ascends to mortality . . .

Now observe how the Canadian poet Archibald Lampman approaches a not dissimilar subject in his sonnet sequence *The Larger Life*:

> I lie upon my bed and hear and see.
> The moon is rising through the glistening trees:
> And momently a great and somber breeze,
> With a vast voice returning, fitfully,
> Comes like a deep-toned grief, and stirs in me,
> Somehow, by some inexplicable art,
> A sense of my soul's strangeness, and its part
> In the dark march of human destiny.
> What am I, then, and what are they that pass
> Yonder, and love and laugh, and mourn and weep?
> What shall they know of me, or I, alas!
> Of them? . . .

Before asking his questions, the author surrounds himself with a suggestive atmosphere, which includes "The moon . . . rising through the glistening trees" and the breeze "With a vast voice returning fitfully." And because of these accessories to beauty—though also to a degree because of the grace of rhyme and meter—Lampman puts one in a mood to share in his meditations. But Miss Moore, opening point-blank with her questions, as directly and no more beautifully than a schoolmistress, creates no mood in which her inquiries can either touch the heart or impress the mind.

§ 2

No matter what the sophisticates may decree, nature goes her old beauty-making way. You may see proofs of this wherever you turn, in great things and in minute: in the majestic brow of a mountain, and the vari-colored pattern of a butterfly's wings; in the nave-like vault of a redwood forest, and the jeweled flash of a humming-bird; in the white glory of a cascading stream, and the dainty purple-yellow of wild iris; in the violet and amethyst continents of sunset cloud, and in a spray of wild fennel, or a thistle leaf streaked with milky white; in the tumult of waves against the cliffs, the commotion of vast winds, the music of rivers, and the song of birds. And you may recognize beauty in the eyes of children, the lithe bodies of youth, the shapes and tints of rose and heliotrope, the gnome-like loveliness of bees, and the innumerable shades, forms, and shadows that give grace and splendor to the desert and the canyon, the prairie and the ocean, the stars and the sky.

Thus surrounded by beauty, thus steeped in it, how can we proclaim that beauty is not, and that henceforth it shall play no part in literature? As successfully might we legislate against eclipses of the moon, or prohibit the rising of the tides. True, the earthworm boring through the soil may not see the eclipse; the ostrich with its head in the sand may deny the reality of tides. But they will still be visible to swallows and skylarks.

Even within ourselves, if we will but let ourselves see it or listen, beauty sparkles and calls, as ancient as the first modeler in clay, as long-lived as the last man. Although hidden or denied, it will reassert itself, it must reassert itself as long as men have generous or soaring thoughts, as long as pines point heavenward in needled green, as long as spring follows winter, and dawns burst into red fire, and suns go down in a smolder of crimson, and stars rise above a world velvet-cloaked with night.

"But even conceding all this," the young poet will cry, "how am I to put beauty into my work? Where and how am I to look for it?" And the answer is that the poet is not to look for beauty; he is to let beauty look for him. And if he gives it the opportunity, he may be sure that beauty will find him. He need but open his mind and his eyes and his heart, and drink in the life that surrounds him; he need but let it flow in over him from the fields and the woods, the waters and the skies, the villages and the cities, and the depths of that inner self in which great poets have always found windows upon reality. Then he will be able to feel, with Shelley, that

> Life, like a dome of many-colored glass,
> Stains the white radiance of eternity.

Then too, with Shelley, he will see

> That Light whose smile kindles the Universe,
> That Beauty in which all things move and work.

He will have something of that experience of the universal half-gropingly expressed by the Irish poet "A. E." when he feels himself uplifted "By a hand of fire . . . To the mystic heart of beauty and the secret of her thought," and sees

> Suns and stars and myriad races
> Mount the spirit spires of beauty, reaching upward
>   to the day
> When the Shepherd of the Ages draws his misty
>   hordes away . . .

What if the poet here clutches amid a mist at something beyond himself, something greater than he can grasp in words? Is not all poetry a process of reaching beyond one's self? But in the case of beauty one need merely open one's eyes, and accept what is given one. He who struggles to obtain beauty will fail, just as he who struggles to be humorous will at best provoke a wry smile. But he whose deeper perceptions are awake, and who feels beauty beating in every pulse and quivering at every nerve-end, will take to beauty as naturally as the wild swan takes to the water. And the beauty that he breathes forth will draw the beauty-loving to him, and will be their final, their most convincing assurance that he is a poet.

IX

"Faery Lands Forlorn"

While most prose says only what it means, the best poetry means more than it says. The poet's eye, "in a fine frenzy rolling," looks not only from heaven to earth and earth to heaven, but from the seen to the unseen, and from the said to the unsaid. Even when the poet's words may be accepted literally and exactly, the implications may reach out endlessly, like sunlight beyond a pond that glitters with its reflections. Thus when Byron speaks of "The Glory and the Nothing of a Name," he is summarizing a philosophy, if not a life experience. And when Milton makes an equally direct statement, in the most unassuming language, "They also serve who only stand and wait," he is saying something as understandably plain as anything he could tell us; but if one considers this line in connection with the rest of the poem and the fact of the poet's blindness, one has boundless suggestions of suffering and endurance, fortitude, resignation, courage and inner adventure.

Two of the best-known lines that, while speaking clearly, say far more than their evident content, are these often quoted ones from Keats:

> . . . magic casements opening on the foam
> Of perilous seas, in faery lands forlorn.

To the imaginative mind, this can conjure forth a whole wonder-world, a world of knights and princes, of fairies and goblins and giants, of charmed adventure and enchanted events. And the same is true of innumerable passages from other poets. Much less known, though moving in the same direction of witchery and romance, are lines such as these from Arthur O'Shaughnessy's *Bisclavaret*:

The splendid fearful herds that stray
 By midnight, when tempestuous moons
Light them to many a shadowy prey,
 And earth beneath the thunder swoons.

Here are suggestions of horror—horror far beyond anything
actually stated. And horror, again exceeding the direct state-
ments almost as a man's shadow may outmeasure the man,
looks out from this in Masefield's *The Hounds of Hell*:

They shook to watch them as they sped,
 All black against the sky;
A horseman with a hooded head
 And great hounds padding by.

Sometimes the suggestions, likewise outtraveling anything
directly stated, may be built up in stanza after stanza. This
is true in Hood's eerie poem *The Haunted House*, in which
the ghostly effects are established through the enumeration of
a long succession of desolate details, such as

With shattered panes the grassy court was starred;
The time-worn coping stone had tumbled after;
And through the ragged roof the sky shone, barred
With naked beam and rafter.

The ruinous state of the house, to be sure, does not logically
prove it to be haunted; but psychologically the conviction of
things grisly and phantasmal fastens itself more and more
upon the reader. And though this may also be the acknowledged method of prose narration, in poetry the effects are
intensified and the suggestions developed beyond anything
possible in prose.

In the opening lines of the "Choric Song" from Tennyson's
The Lotos-Eaters, the same method of suggestion is used to

produce an opposite impression: that of softness, languor and
lassitude:

> There is sweet music here that softer falls
> Than petals from blown roses on the grass,
> Or night-dews on still waters between walls
> Of shadowy granite, in a gleaming pass;
> Music that gentlier on the spirit lies
> Than tired eyelids upon tired eyes . . .

Again, the poet means more than he says. And the things
unsaid may be the very ones that stimulate and bewitch.

A suggestiveness of a different type, more concise but as
revealing as shafts of sunlight shot through the crannies of a
shuttered house, are these lines from the opening of Meredith's *Modern Love*:

> . . . looking through their dead blank years,
> By vain regret scrawled over the blank wall.
> Like sculptured effigies they might be seen
> Upon their marriage-tomb, the sword between;
> Each wishing for the sword that severs all.

One has been told little specifically. And yet, in a sense—
and particularly through the deft references to the sword—one
has been told all.

The same is true when, later in the sequence, Meredith
utters these lines:

> Ah, what a dusty answer gets the soul
> When hot for certainties in this our life!

It would be hard to compress more of a man's philosophy
into two lines. But again the real meaning is not so much in
the words as in the illumination behind the words. Those of
us who feel we have had a "dusty answer" . . . "when hot for

certainties" will be able to elaborate pages of response. And those who have not had the experience will none the less feel a stirring of interest, of wonder or curiosity, or perhaps of protest or dissent.

And how much may be said in a few simple lyrical lines, such as those that conclude Felicia Hemans' *Dirge*:

> They that have seen thy look in death
> No more may fear to die.

And what sardonic connotations, what an essay on the irony and futility of glory in the fourteen lines of Shelley's *Ozymandias*, with the shattered image of the proud and sneering face lying in the desert beside "two vast and trunkless legs of stone," and with the imperious inscription of the "king of kings," leading toward the conclusion:

> Nothing beside remains. Round the decay
> Of that colossal wreck, boundless and bare
> The lone and level sands stretch far away.

In such work, poetry fulfills itself. While speaking clearly, it overflows the actual words as a fountain overflows its source.

§ 2

When poetry does not, as in these examples, speak with a single voice that is yet many voices, it tends to fall toward the flats of prose. This is one reason why poets of the school of Pope and Dryden are not generally credited with being as poetic as their great predecessors and successors. Take these lines by De Foe (who, though esteemed as a poet by his contemporaries, has been valued by later generations only for his prose):

> Whenever God erects a House of Prayer
> The Devil always builds a chapel there.

> And 'twill be found upon examination
> The latter has the largest congregation.

There is a cleverness, a satirical bite in these lines, but little more. One is not thrilled with a sense of unexplored hinterlands, a feeling of unpenetrated depths within the life of the author or the spirit of man. De Foe says what he says, and says it without hints or adumbrations of seductive realms beyond. He has given us, in other words, little more than rhymed prose, though prose made sharper and more pointed by the poetic tools of rhyme and meter.

The failings thus exemplified by De Foe, who was following in the rut of the driest, most uninspired school known to English poetry between Chaucer's day and our own, have been duplicated and multiplied by the exponents of the "new" in poetry, beginning with Whitman. Certainly, there are no hints of "lamps beyond the sunset" or "The light that never was on sea or land" in lines such as these from the renowned Walt's apostrophe to the body:

> I believe the likes of you shall stand or fall with my
>   poems, and that they are my poems,
> Man's, woman's, child's, youth's, wife's, husband's, mother's,
>   father's, young man's, young woman's poems,
> Head, neck, hair, ears, drop and tympan of the ears,
> Eyes, eye-fringes, iris of the eyes, eyebrows, and the
>   waking or sleeping of the lids,
> Mouth, tongue, lips, teeth, roof of the mouth, jaws,
>   and the jaw hinges . . .

It is needless to continue through the many more lines listing anatomical features. From all the above, it will be seen that Whitman leaves about as much unsaid as a textbook on physiology, and writes in about the alluring style of a mail-order catalogue. Instead of a "fine excess," he gives us a gross excess. By leaving nothing unsaid, he leaves nothing said poetically. There are no "faery lands forlorn" and no "magic casements," because there is no magic. There is merely the barefaced prose of everyday, without a flash or glimmer of any realm but that of everyday, and without a suggestion of any depth in man beneath "flakes of breast-muscle, pliant backbone and neck, flesh not flabby, good-sized arms and legs" (which, if you substitute "wings" for "arms," sounds like a good description of a Thanksgiving turkey).

True, the author does mention "passions, desires, reachings, aspirations." But to mention such abstractions is not to give them hue and substance as a creative reality. It is merely to follow the method of the newspaper reporter—or of the dictionary.

Yet this method of Whitman, so destructive of poetic values because it means no more than it says and casts no suggestive glitters, is the method adopted by most practitioners of so-called "modernism." We have seen this in many of the quotations made in these pages; but in order to refresh the reader's memory, I may mention lines such as these by Edgar Lee Masters, the once widely acclaimed but now little mentioned author of *The Spoon River Anthology*:

Where are Elmer, Herman, Bert, Tom, and Charley,
The weak of will, the strong of arm, the clown, the
    boozer, the fighter?
All, all are sleeping on the hill.

These questions bring reminders of Villon's *Ballade of the Lords of Old Time*, and even more so of the *Ballade of Dead Ladies*, with its rhetorical questions as to the whereabouts of various fair ones, such as "Lady Flora, the lovely Roman." But the latter is elevated into poetry by the suggestive refrain, "Where are the snows of yesteryear?", whereas Masters' repeated "All, all are sleeping on the hill" has about the same

poetic overtones as a radio announcer's reiterated advice to buy
Macrae's Old Scotch Whisky.

Now take this example, by Archibald MacLeish:

> Fish has laid her succulent eggs
> Safe in Sargasso weed
> So wound and bound with crabbed legs
> No clattering claws can find and feed.

Despite the rhymes, this is much less poetic to my mind
than the following:

> The honeybee goes forth from the hive in spring
> Like the dove from Noah's ark.
> And it is not until after many days
> That she brings back the olive leaf.

However, the latter passage was not originally printed as
above. Instead, it appears thus:

> The honeybee goes forth from the hive in spring like the
> dove from Noah's ark, and it is not until after many days
> that she brings back the olive leaf.

You may find this passage at the opening of John Burrough's
essay on *Insect and Amphibian Ways*.* Please note that it con-
tains intimations of things beyond the spoken word, and hence
has some of the qualities of poetry, whereas the passage by
MacLeish merely says what it has to say, and therefore follows
the method of journalistic prose.

Let us take another example. I quote from Robert Penn
Warren's *To A Little Girl, One Year Old, In A Ruined
Fortress*:

------

* *John Burroughs' America. Selections from the Writings of the
Hudson River Naturalist*, New York, 1951.

The child next door is defective because the mother,
Seven brats already in that purlieu of dirt,
Took a pill, or did something to herself she thought
    would not hurt,
But it did, and no good, for there came this monstrous
    other.

Here a human tragedy is described in terms as unilluminating as an account of the latest sordid murder intrigue in this morning's paper. Consider by contrast this treatment of a human theme by another poet of our age, Siegfried Sassoon:

His headstrong thoughts that once in eager strife
Leapt sure from eye to brain and back to eye,
Weaving unconscious tapestries of life,
Are now thrust inward, dungeoned from the sky.
    And he who has watched the world and loved it all,
    Starless and old and blind, a sight for pity,
    With feeble steps and fingers on the wall,
    Gropes with his staff along the rumbling city.*

There is a picture here, from which the mind may elaborate other pictures almost endlessly; there are pathos and pity, which burst upon us with a force beyond that of the individual words; there is a life-story, told by the silences within the lines almost more than by the lines themselves. In short, there is a poem.

Now consider one of the modern writings about poetry. I take these lines from Wallace Stevens' *Of Modern Poetry*:

It has to be living, to learn the speech of the place.
It has to face the men of the time and to meet
The women of the time. It has to think about war
And it has to find what will suffice. It has
To construct a new stage. It has to be on that stage . . .

*From *Collected Poems* (1949), by permission of The Viking Press, Inc.

Compare this with a passage by another writer:

He must at the same time bewitch us through our senses
And the poetry must enter, if at all, through our nerves
As well as through our brains. The sense of the poem
Has to be imparted through its sound—and the sound
Will include meter, stanza, pattern, and rhyme
As well as phrase and the chiming of word against word.

Which is the more poetic? Personally, I see little to choose
from the poetic point of view; each makes some direct state-
ments, and nothing more; and neither attunes our ears to the
echoes that roll in from the void, nor to the vibrations beyond
ordinary sight. The first, however, was originally printed as
above; the second was presented as prose in the opening chapter of Theodore Maynard's critical volume, *Preface to Poetry*.*

§ 3

For want of a better term, critics have used the word "magic"
to describe that quality in poetry which transports the reader
outside himself, which sows suggestions and weaves an en-
chantment over the imagination, and which says much by saying little. There is magic in some of the quotations made a few
pages back, as in the reference by Keats to "perilous seas in
faery lands forlorn." And there is magic in much of the work
of twentieth century and classical poets. Other examples are
to be found in de la Mare's

"Is there anybody there?" said the Traveller,
Knocking on the moonlit door,

and in Bridges'

Whither, O splendid ship, thy white sails crowding,
Leaning across the bosom of the urgent West?

* Theodore Maynard, *Preface to Poetry*, New York, 1933.

And there is magic in the mood evoked by Arnold's *Philomela*:

> Hark! ah, the nightingale—
> The tawny-throated!
> Hark, from that moonlit cedar what a burst!
> What triumph! hark! — what pain!

Magic invests the concluding lines of a quatrain on *The Absolute*, by a contemporary writer, Hugh Wilgus Ramsaur:

> No vaster, holding all Eternity,
> Than one pale petal fading in your hands.

True, we do have reminders here of Blake's quatrain beginning, "To see the world in a grain of sand," but the resemblance is not so close as to prevent Mr. Ramsaur's lines from suggesting a whole new concept of reality.

Again we have magic, with connotations of the cosmic, in the opening of Eric Barker's sonnets on *Point Lobos, California*:

> Here Time is God: his shadow on this land
> Lies dark across the cypress and the stone.

Or consider the following, by another contemporary, Otto Freund:

> The wound is healed, but still the pain is there,
>   And stabs with anguish, like a sudden sword,
> When sunlight feigns the spun gold of her hair,
>   Or music finds her lost voice in a chord.

What worlds here of seductiveness and love, of longing and heartbreak and tragedy, all within four simply worded lines!

To take a final example: here are the concluding lines of

George Sterling's sonnet *Kindred*, in which he stands at the seashore, "Musing, between the sunset and the dark":

> There sank the sun Arcturus, and I thought:
> Star, by an ocean on a world of thine,
> May not a being, born, like me, to die,
> Confront a little the eternal Naught
> And watch our isolated sun decline—
> Sad for his evanescence, even as I?

Again, what implications! What worlds for the mind and imagination! Once more the author has magically transcended his own words.

But a theme, in order to contain magic, need not be philosophical like this sonnet by Sterling, nor eerie like de la Mare's *The Listeners*, nor cosmic like the quatrain by H. W. Ramsaur, nor stately like Bridges' lines on the ship. Into almost any theme, a writer of talent can inject magic, provided only that he himself glows with feeling for his subject-matter. Some themes—as, for example, that of *The Ancient Mariner* or of *Kulba Khan* or *A Midsummer Night's Dream* or *The Tempest* or *The Eve of St. Agnes*—seem to have magic inherent in them, though it takes a most skilled hand to bring it out. But the able writer can pour magic even into subjects that might seem unpromising. This is what Edwin Markham, for example, has done with *The Man With the Hoe*, who stands before us "Bowed by the weight of centuries," almost an heroic figure. This is what Oscar Wilde has accomplished in *The Ballad of Reading Gaol*, in which he has woven lines of magic even out of the grimness of prison life and the ghastliness of the death penalty. This is what Thomas Hood has achieved in *The Dream of Eugene Aram*, another long ballad, in which a tale of sordid murder is told in a way that throws a glow over the telling. And this is what the too-little remembered writer John Davidson has contrived to do in some of his nar-

ratives, such as *A Ballad of Heaven,* in which a composer living in a garret "wrought at one great work for years," until
the masterpiece was completed and his wife and child lay dead;
after which he followed them to Heaven, "where systems
whirling stand, / Where galaxies like snow are driven," and
after various adventures was greeted with the reassurance that,

> The music that you made below
> Is now the music of the spheres.

In order to create "the music of the spheres," one must
inject magic; and in order to inject magic, one must utilize
every weapon in the poetic arsenal. One must—to recapitu-
late—attain mastery over meter and rhyme, and know when
the latter is demanded, and when it may be omitted; one
must have an understanding of the uses and abuses of words,
and be able to distinguish between truth and dictatorial rules
and tabus; one must learn to keep one's windows clean, and to
express one's thoughts and moods as clearly as the nature of
the subject-matter makes possible; one must recognize that
the head must never eclipse the heart, and that much of poetry
is and always has been of the emotions; one must not strain
for originality lest one end in bombast or bathos, but must
quietly work within the limits of the gifts given by nature;
and one must pay reverence to the ever-burning lamp of beauty.

Only so can one master one's craft. Only so can one write
poetry—that poetry which, as Edwin Markham puts it, "comes
like the husht beauty of the night, / And sees too deep for
laughter," that poetry which has been "a vibration and a light,"
an inspiration and a joy to countless generations, and which,
if the measure of man's accomplishment were to be taken
among the high gods, would undoubtedly be accounted one
of his chief claims to glory and to an eventual seat among
the angels.

THE END